APR 1 '93

DATE DUE		
APR 1 5 '93	FEB 13 '99	
MAY 0 1 '93	MAY 17 '99	
JUN 1 8 '93	APR 11 '00	
DEC 1 3 '93	AUG 30 '00	
JUL 0 2 '94	AUG 06 '03	
AUG 09 '94	JUN 02 '04	
APR 28 '95	NO 62 90V	
APR 2 9 '96		
AUG 2 8 '96		
OCT 0 9 '96		
JA 29 '98		
MAY 26 '98		

Jackson
County
Library
System

HEADQUARTERS:

413 W. Main

Medford, Oregon   97501

A TEEN'S GUIDE TO BUSINESS

The Secrets to a Successful Enterprise

LINDA MENZIES
OREN S. JENKINS
RICKELL RAE FISHER

MasterMedia Limited • New York

MASTERMEDIA and colophon are registered
trademarks of MasterMedia Limited.

Library of Congress Cataloging-in-Publication Data
Menzies, Linda.
    A teen's guide to business : the secrets to a successful enterprise / Linda
Menzies, Oren S. Jenkins, Rickell R. Fisher.
       p.   cm.
    Summary: Offers advice on such topics as how to find the right job, create
a better product or service, develop a business plan, and deal with money
matters.
    ISBN 0-942361-50-4
    1. Success in business—Juvenile literature.   2. Entrepreneurship—Juvenile
literature.   3. Creative ability in business—Juvenile literature.
[1. Entrepreneurship.   2. Business enterprises.   3. Vocational guidance.]
I. Jenkins, Oren S.   II. Fisher, Rickell R.   III. Title.
HF5392.M46   1992
650.1—dc20   92-4223
                                                                      CIP
                                                                      AC

Manufactured in the United States of America

CONTENTS

Contents

INTRODUCTION

If you picked up this book, chances are you want to find an after-school or summer job—or you're interested in starting your own business. You know that by working you can:

- earn money to pay for part (and, in some cases, *all*) of your college tuition;
- make enough money to buy an expensive stereo system, or your first car, or a great new wardrobe;
- learn on-the-job skills that will give you a head start on your post-college career; and
- gain confidence and high self-esteem (not to mention respect from friends and family) by proving you've got what it takes to make it in the business world.

But, like most teens, you probably have a lot of questions and concerns, such as:

- How can I find a good job that fits into my school (and social) schedule?
- How can I find out what type of job I'm suited for?
- Will I need a résumé—and how can I put together a "professional" résumé if I've never held a *real* job?
- How should I dress for an interview?
- How do I prepare for an interview—is there a certain way I should act? What questions can I expect? What should I do to keep from getting nervous?
- When I *do* land a job, how should I dress for work? How should I act in order to get a raise? A promotion?
- I'm interested in starting my own business—but how do I know if I'll be able to pull it off and handle the pressure?

The three of us got *our* first jobs—or started businesses—through trial and error. Looking back, we realize we could have used a comprehensive "guide to business," a book that talked to teens only, that gave us practical how-tos for making it in the work world. That's why we decided to write this book—to make *your* first business experience a little easier. First, we'll tell you about ourselves and the work we've done (between the three of us, we've held approximately 14 jobs!). Then, in following chapters, we'll answer your questions about careers for teens. We'll tell you how to mount a job campaign, and share "interview techniques." We'll show you how to put together an impressive résumé that draws on your school (and volunteer) experiences. We'll give you tips for keeping your social life alive and well, and for managing stress, while you juggle school and work. And, for aspiring entrepreneurs—those of you who want to start and run your own businesses—we'll explain how to set up a workable business plan, where to find customers, how to advertise your product or service, and much more.

We'll also introduce you to some enterprising teens from across the U.S.A.: a guy who worked for a veterinarian, and is now in a pre-vet program in college; a girl who waitresses at Pizza Hut and can explain why waiting tables at a fast-food restaurant beats working at an upscale establishment; a guy who drives an ambulance and is getting on-the-job experience that will prepare him for a career in medicine; a 13-year-old who invented a biodegradable golf tee, then founded his own company; a teen who owns and runs a successful computer instruction firm and charges between $30 and $40 an hour for his services.

One of the hottest (and smartest) trends of the '90s is teens going to work and *starting* businesses. What's more, work can be exciting, challenging—and just plain fun. Read through this book. Fill in the work sheets. Take the quizzes. Really *think* about what you want to do now—and in the future. Then, like us, you can go out and land that terrific job—or launch your own super-successful, moneymaking company!

LINDA:

I started working when I was 16 and had just graduated from high school. I was a part-time graphic designer for a man who invented kids' toys, furniture and various travel items; my job was creating the packaging for his merchandise. I've been drawing since I was a little kid, so essentially, I turned my hobby—my love of art—into my vocation. Eventually, I decided to study design and photography, as well as computer graphics, in college.

During college, I sold Avon products on campus (my mom's an Avon Representative, too, so I learned the "basics" from her). I made $60,000 in just three years and was able to pay for most of my room and board, and tuition, as well as my expensive photography equipment. I used my art and computer graphics background to advertise my Avon business, creating colorful signs I posted around the campus. As word spread that I sold Avon products, my customers literally came to *me!*

After graduating from college (at 19), I found a job at a Miami silk-screening company that manufactured tee shirts for national and international clients. I started as a graphic designer and assistant to the owner, but he liked my work so much he promoted me to art director within six months. Suddenly, I had a tremendous amount of responsibility—supervising the other designers, coming up with ideas for new tee shirt designs, making certain that during the silk-screening process the colors turned out exactly right.

We designed all sorts of tee shirts—"souvenir" tees, shirts for various arts festivals, tees for sports teams and events, including the International Soccer Championships—and I was responsible for developing four to six designs a day.

Having so much responsibility early on at the company (and at such a young age) gave me the confidence I needed to go out on my own. In my spare time, I began doing freelance work, including designing the souvenir tee for a big arts festival held every year in Miami Beach. I'd attended the festival for several years and felt I could design a *better* tee than the one the festival committee sold—one that incorporated *all* elements of the festival, including art, music, and dance. So I submitted a half dozen ideas to the committee. They liked my work and commissioned me to design the official tee for the festival. Sending in my ideas was a risk—but a small one. I had nothing to lose and everything to gain.

Today, I'm a freelance photographer and graphic designer, running my own company, Linda, Linda Productions. My father owns a business in Central America, so I'm able to travel there often and frequently do photography and design work for various consulates. I shoot photos for travel brochures, and I've worked with the consulate for tourism and Minister of Foreign Affairs for Belize (a small country near Mexico), designing souvenir tees for tourists. I gained a great deal of confidence by selling Avon, so I'm comfortable making presentations to delegations from various consulates to explain why *my* tee shirts are superior in design and quality to those they've bought previously.

My next career move? Soon, I'll begin studying film production at the Pratt Institute (a prestigious art school in New York City). I plan to become a documentary filmmaker.

OREN:

I was a high school freshman when I came up with the idea of starting my own lawn service. I'd noticed that many of the people in my neighborhood were elderly and couldn't take care of their lawns. Other lawn services in our area were expensive—charging $50 and up just to cut grass and trim hedges.

I figured I could offer quality service for less, charging $20 for everything from cutting grass to pruning bushes to raking leaves. And, unlike the *established* lawn services, I promised my customers I'd care for their lawns at *any* time (even if I had to break social commitments to do it!). I tended an average of seven lawns a week, before school, after school, in the evenings, and on Saturdays and Sundays. It was a major undertaking—many nights I'd fall into bed totally exhausted because I'd stayed up until 1 or 2 A.M. studying (I maintained a B+/A − average, and also managed to play varsity basketball).

My business grew through "word of mouth" recommendations. If one customer was happy with my work, he'd recommend me to a friend. So when the economy slowed down in the late '80s and early '90s, and the commercial lawn services started losing customers, *my* business was going strong—in part because I offered excellent service at a reduced rate.

I brought in about $160 a week (I used some of my initial profits to buy a good power mower and hedge trimmer, but otherwise, I had no "overhead" costs). Most of my money went into my college fund.

I liked being self-employed, but I also wanted more "people contact." And, I wanted to work in a corporation where I could move up the ladder and learn solid business skills. During my junior year in high school, I took a job as a ride attendant at Kings Island Amusement Park, near Cincinnati, Ohio. I was responsible for seating kids and adults on the King Cobra Roller Coaster and making sure they obeyed the safety rules. I earned a reputation for being friendly to the public, as well as reliable and conscientious, so the summer before I started college, my employers asked me to work in the "money room." This was a wonderful compliment since I was the first summer employee—and the only teen—to be promoted to work in this area. (Usually, adults from the accounting department handled all the money responsibilities).

My money room duties included counting daily receipts in excess of $10,000, producing a daily computerized revenue report, supplying change for all the cash registers in the park, depositing money, and balancing money for daily receipts.

I learned a lot from running my own lawn service and working

Kings Island. The lawn service taught me discipline, and how to make the customer happy." At Kings Island, I learned how to manage money, the need for accuracy, and the ability to concentrate on highly detailed work.

Today, I'm an accounting major at Ohio Wesleyan University—and thanks to those early job experiences, I think I have a real head start on a successful career in business.

RICKELL:

My first work experience was as a volunteer—a candy striper—at a local hospital when I was 13. I dealt with the patients on a personal basis, talking with them, bringing them magazines and meal trays. My job was to help the hospital staff *and* make the patients feel more comfortable. It was a great experience: I learned how to present or explain things to others in an entirely different way than I was used to. For example, one of the patients was a blind man who needed help with his meal tray. I explained that his chicken was at the "12 o'clock" position on the plate, his peas at the "3 o'clock" spot, and so on. In working with him and the other patients, I learned to explain things clearly and patiently—and to be flexible, to change my own thinking about things. This has helped me tremendously in my other jobs. I also learned to really *listen* to people, to discover their needs and wants. Again, this has been an invaluable tool in business.

I spent two years working part time at the hospital, then for the next two years, I worked as a babysitter for my neighbor. My first "real" job was at a fast-food restaurant called RAX, where I started out behind the counter, but was eventually moved to the cash register, where I was taking orders, dealing with money, and meeting the public. Soon, I was promoted to head cashier. I learned very quickly how to deal with the various customers—some people were in great moods, others weren't so positive. It was my job to make them feel welcome. I enjoyed learning how to "read" a customer, then trying to make him or her feel a little happier if they happened to be in a crummy mood. I'd compliment a woman on her blouse, for example. Being nice to the customers made *me* feel good about what I was doing—and my bosses liked my approach.

After a year and a half at RAX (working after school and summers), I got a job at a family-owned restaurant where I was a jack-of-all-trades. I waitressed, I cleaned up, I even helped the cook.

The summer after I graduated from high school, I landed a job at a car dealership, working in the customer service department. Because of my hospital and restaurant experience, I was comfortable dealing with the public, and I made follow-up calls to customers to make sure they were satisfied with the service they'd received. I was at the dealership for only one month when Pittsburgh Plate Glass (PPG) offered me a terrific job in the plant. (I'd made minimum wage at my other jobs and PPG hired me at $8.50 an hour; if the PPG job hadn't come along, I probably wouldn't have earned enough money to go to college!)

Working at the glass plant was a unique experience. As a "summer wareroom utility worker," I did everything from working on the production line, to inspecting glass for defects, to operating a forklift. And I learned a lot about discipline and hard work. I worked eight-hour shifts, 40 hours a week, plus overtime. Often, I was on the "graveyard shift," and weeks might go by when I didn't have a weekend off.

But I missed working directly with the public—our "customer" at PPG was a sticker on a piece of glass. So after two summers, I decided to take a job as a customer service rep at a department store, and in my spare time, I sold Avon products. I sold to my co-workers *and* covered a territory near my home, selling door-to-door. Looking back, I wish I'd devoted *all* my time to selling Avon—the market was there, and I could have developed a huge customer base and made a tremendous amount of money.

Today, I'm a junior at Indiana University of Pennsylvania, majoring in media and communications. My goal? A career in corporate communications—dealing with the public, of course!

Linda Menzies, 21, Miami Beach, Florida
Oren S. Jenkins, 19, Cincinnati, Ohio
Rickell Rae Fisher, 20, Franklin, Pennsylvania

A Teen's Guide to Business

1

A World of Possibilities

You've decided you want to go to work—to earn money, to get a leg up on the career of your dreams, or to just get a feel for the world of business and where *you* fit in. But how do you start? The possibilities seem endless!

You *could* go to work for "Corporate America"—by that we mean those businesses, large or small, publicly or family-run, that employ thousands of teens in summer and afterschool jobs. Your mom or dad may work for a corporation, so you probably already know a little about the pros and cons. Whether you work as a file clerk at a major manufacturing plant or as a counter person at a fast-food restaurant, you'll need to consider what working for someone else, what reporting to a boss (or bosses) means:

THE PLUSES

- You'll get a regular paycheck—unless you're in a job such as waiting tables, where a major part of your income is made up of tips—and you'll know *exactly* how much money you can expect to make every week.
- You'll meet new people—not just other kids like yourself, but adults who can show you the ropes, teach you the business, act as your "mentors."
- You'll get on-the-job training and learn new skills that will be valuable when you look for that post-college job.

- If you work hard, and your bosses like you, you can be assured of excellent references (for those all-important college applications *and* future jobs).
- Unless you're doing shift work, or are "on call" at odd hours, your work schedule will be set and your time off will be your own.
- You'll feel proud because you're earning your own money—and you'll garner the respect of family, co-workers, and friends because of the terrific job you're doing.

THE MINUSES

- No corporate job—not even summer and part-time work—is completely guaranteed these days. It's *likely* that if you sign on to work June, July and August, you'll be with the company the entire time. But if massive layoffs or cutbacks take place, or the company posts record losses rather than profits, you *could* find yourself job hunting by mid-July.
- As a 9-to-5 summer employee, or afterschool parttimer, your time on the job is not your own. Your boss will expect you to report to work on time, and stay until you're scheduled to head home. That means no sleeping in, no taking a day off to go to the beach, no calling in sick because you've got a major English lit paper due the next day.
- Just as your time isn't your own, neither is the decision of how you'll spend it on the job yours. You were hired to do certain tasks—which you may or may not enjoy. You have to answer to your bosses and, for the most part, do things the way *they* want you to do them.
- You may find you've taken on a schedule that's too demanding—and your schoolwork, extracurricular activities, and social life are being moved to a back burner. You

may also feel stressed out from trying to work 4 P.M. to 8 P.M. every day, then rushing home to study for a big chem exam.

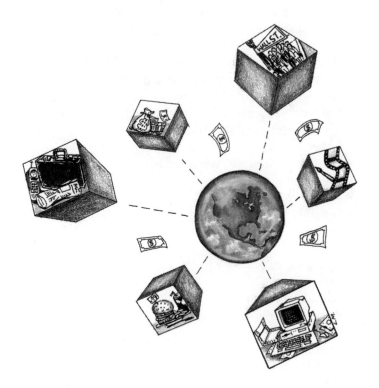

OKAY, YOU WANT A JOB—SO WHERE ARE THEY?

Every business is your potential employer. Just look around you. Numerous corporations sponsor afterschool or summer "internship" programs for high school and college students, and many businesses like to hire and train teens (in the hope that those kids will return to fill full-time slots after they finish college).

Below is a list of *just a few* of the many places you can look for work:

- Major corporations and manufacturing plants
- Small businesses (doctors' offices, dental clinics, law offices, travel agencies, flower shops, computer stores, bicycle repair shops, landscaping and lawn services, sports equipment stores, hardware and appliance stores—many hire clerical, repair or sales help)
- Fast-food restaurants (the bread-and-butter work—no pun intended—of many teens)
- Coffee shops
- Family and "upscale" restaurants
- Delis
- Meat and fish markets
- Gourmet food stores
- Ice cream and frozen yogurt shops
- Bakeries
- Candy stores
- Grocery stores
- Amusement parks
- Parks and recreation services
- Health clubs and gyms
- Golf courses
- Service stations
- Kennels
- Pet stores
- Animal hospitals
- People hospitals
- Nursing homes
- Shoe stores

- Department stores
- Specialty stores (such as Benetton and The Gap)
- Discount outlets
- Children's clothing shops
- Libraries
- Schools (working in the administration office)
- Day-care centers and toddler playgroups
- Summer camps

ANOTHER OPTION—STARTING YOUR *OWN* BUSINESS

While it may seem that going to work for a corporation or small business is the logical thing to do (after all, that's what your friends, and your brothers and sisters have done—right?), there *is* another way to get your start in the business world. More and more, teens are launching their own businesses. Like many of their adult counterparts, kids are rediscovering an early American tradition: that pioneer spirit of doing things for themselves. With intelligence and hard work—and a good idea—teens all across the country (and around the world, for that matter) are taking control of their lives and becoming successful entrepreneurs making $10,000, $20,000—even $50,000 a year.

Sounds too good to be true? A teenager with his or her own business. It happens every day. Just look at 17-year-old Julian Riedlbauer, a German teen we recently read about in *The Wall Street Journal.* When he was 15, Julian started his own computer business by buying 10 Taiwanese-made modems for $1,200 (he borrowed the money from his dad), then *reselling* them by mail at a 30 percent markup. Today, he sells computer equipment on two continents, has approximately 300 customers, and projected sales of more than $300,000 in 1991.

Then there's 15-year-old David Eilers of Marietta, Georgia, who runs a successful lawn service that brought in $50,000 in revenues in 1990 (he projected earnings at close to $100,000 in 1991). And there's 16-year-old Lana Israel of Miami, Florida, who, at 14, wrote an innovative book about a new learning technique and now runs her own publishing company. (We'll tell you more about David and Lana later).

The '90s truly are the decade of the entrepreneur. As companies continue to downsize and jobs fall by the wayside, becoming your own boss—and relying on your own motivation, making your own luck—seems to be the way to go for many teens. Here are the major pros and cons of becoming an entrepreneur:

THE PLUSES

- *You* determine your work hours, make your schedule—and fit your work around school, family and social commitments.
- You don't have to take orders from a boss.
- You set your own wages.
- You determine your earnings, depending on how motivated you are, how hard you work—and how well you know your market.
- You learn the ins and outs of the business world light-years ahead of other kids, who won't enter the work force until after college.
- You'll make new contacts—friends, customers, and businesspeople—who can help you in later years.

THE MINUSES

- You take a risk whenever you go into business for yourself; if you don't make the right decisions, or get the best advice, you *could* lose your capital (the money you spent up front to get into business).

- You'll have times—even though your hours are flexible—when you may have to work late, or on weekends, or say "no" to social engagements.
- You don't have to answer to a boss, but you do have to answer to your customers. If a customer isn't satisfied, you'll have to replace the product you sold him, or redo the work.
- You'll spend part of your time dealing with paperwork (keeping detailed records of your business costs and income, preparing tax returns).
- You'll have to make your own decisions—no one else (a supervisor or co-worker) will do it for you.
- You'll have only yourself to depend on—unless you hire employees—and you'll work alone. Many self-employed people feel "isolated," even lonely at times, without feedback from a supervisor and daily interaction with fellow workers.
- You must be self-disciplined and self-motivated.
- You won't have a guaranteed paycheck to count on. You may have a terrific month when you seem to "rake in" the money, followed by a slow one, when you make little or nothing at all.
- You may face long hours—and you may feel overwhelmed by the amount of work you have to do (in addition to managing *schoolwork*).
- You must "grow" your business; if it grows slowly, you'll need to deal with feelings of discouragement, while coming up with new strategies for boosting sales.

Still interested in launching your own business? Stop reading now, and turn to page 75, and take our quiz. After you've done that, *and* checked out all the info on starting a new business, *be sure to flip back* to the chapters on "Managing Stress" and "Taking

Control of Your Life." You'll need to do both if you plan to become a successful entrepreneur!

Decided to give Corporate America a try first? The next few chapters will give you important information you'll need to go after, land, and keep a job.

2

Do What You Love . . .

Someone once said, "Do what you love and you'll be a success."
It's true: If you enjoy your work, you'll perform better, please your
bosses, work well with colleagues, and make your customers
happy. (On the other hand, if you *hate* your job, you may be
tempted to show up late, slough off, and count the minutes until
the workday's over.)

Many teens use summer and afterschool jobs to give them an
insider's look—and a head start—on the careers of their dreams.

HIS "OFFICE" IS AN AMBULANCE
*Twenty-year-old Sal DiMeglio is a freshman in the premed program
at Fordham University, in the Bronx, New York. But for the past two
years, he's spent most of his "out-of-school" time in an ambulance.
At 18, Sal decided to take a six-month course to get his EMT
(emergency medical technician) license so he could earn money
for college and get a firsthand look at medicine. Not content to
simply study the basics of EMT work, Sal convinced two of his
instructors to hire him as a part-time ambulance driver. "While I
was learning in class how to use oxygen equipment, and do various
procedures like bandaging, splinting and controlling bleeding, I got
to watch actual EMTs at work. By the time I got my license, I already
had a good overview of the job. The other people in my class had
the knowledge, but they hadn't applied it to real-life situations."*

Sal became so interested in EMT work, he temporarily withdrew from Fordham. "I loved the work and grabbed any shift I could, putting in 60 to 70 hours a week, working midnight to 8 A.M., 4 P.M. to midnight, or 8 P.M. to 4 A.M. The schedule could be grueling—but the excitement and fast pace made up for that."

After watching paramedics in action, Sal was eager to do what they did. "Paramedics are the next level up—they do what EMTs do, as well as more technical things like inserting breathing tubes, placing people on respirators, using a defibrillator (a device that shoots an electrical current through the heart to get it started beating), giving intravenous drugs. Basically, paramedics run a mini-emergency room in an ambulance, getting the patient stabilized before he reaches the hospital."

Sal took the yearlong paramedic course when he was 19 and became the "youngest medic in the county." Paramedic work is great, he says. "I do things in the ambulance a third- or fourth-year medical student hasn't done. I'm getting an incredible amount of experience in the field I want to be in. I've gotten a real 'overview' of medicine; I've done everything from treating cardiac, trauma and burn patients to delivering babies.

"I also get to interact with specialists in every field. When we bring a patient into emergency, a specialist comes down to talk with the patient, so I'm getting a feel for the different specialties, the type of doctor I want to become." Another plus: Sal has become friends with many doctors at the various hospitals in his area. "Many of the doctors are on boards at medical schools, and I'll be able to get letters of recommendation from them when I apply to med school."

Sal reentered the premed program at Fordham last year, but doesn't plan to give up paramedic work any time soon. "I love it. You get such an adrenaline rush in this type of work. It's made me realize that when I do become a doctor, I'll have to work in an area like the emergency room (E.R.). Once you work the streets, you get used to everything happening bam-bam-bam. In the E.R., the atmosphere is the same; the E.R. doctors know that although things *are slow for the moment,* anything *could happen in the next second."*

PART-TIME JOBS THAT LEAD TO CAREERS

It's definitely possible to find a summer or afterschool job that will give you an inside look at your ideal career. Here's a mini-list of careers, matched with part-time jobs that provide valuable experience:

If you want to be:	*Look for a job at:*
a doctor, nurse, lab technician, radiographer, physical or speech therapist, or any other type of health-care worker	a hospital, community health clinic, doctor's office, dental office, pharmacy, nursing home, school for handicapped kids, adult day-care center
a teacher	a school administration office, day-care center, tot drop, private pre-school or kindergarten
a writer, editor or reporter	a local newspaper or magazine, the communications or public affairs department of a corporation, a non-profit organization that publishes a newsletter
a restaurant owner, chef, nutritionist	a restaurant, the food service department of a hospital or nursing home, a university cafeteria or food service, gourmet food store, health food store

If you want to be:	*Look for a job at:*
a sales representative	a department store (or any store where your main duties are sales), a direct-sales company, where you sell door-to-door, at parties, or by phone
a public relations specialist	a public relations (P.R.) or advertising firm, the P.R. or public affairs department of a corporation, the community affairs department at a university, the sales or customer service department of any store
a graphic designer	a graphic design, advertising, or P.R. firm, the graphic design department at a major department or discount store, a local magazine or newspaper
a photographer	a portrait studio, local newspaper or magazine, university photo department

If you have an inkling of the kind of work you'd like to pursue after college, do what we did: make a list of all the places that hire people who go into your particular field of interest, then apply for jobs at those businesses.

Let's say you want to become a hospital lab technician. You apply for a "go-fer" job at your local hospital, and end up running specimens from the emergency room down to the lab. You'll get to know the lab techs and see firsthand what they do. You'll find out whether the work *really* appeals to you before you commit to a long (and often costly) training period. (Rickell Fisher wanted to become a nurse, so she volunteered at her local hospital. "I loved the work," she says, "but when we lost one of our patients, I realized I wasn't cut out to be a nurse. I'm glad I found out then that nursing wasn't the career for me—*before* I spent four years in a nursing program.")

HIS PATIENTS ARE CATS AND DOGS

"I knew early on that I'd like to become a veterinarian," says 18-year-old Keith Weingardt, a freshman majoring in animal science at Cornell University, in Ithaca, New York. "So when I was 14, I asked our local vet, Michael Woltz, if I could work for him part-time. Dr. Woltz knew me and was aware of my interest in animals. We'd taken our dog to his hospital for years and I'd come along when my mom brought her in for shots or various treatments."

Keith worked at Central Animal Hospital for three years after school and during summers. "I worked three weekday shifts, from 3 to 7 P.M., and on Saturdays from 8 A.M. to 3 P.M., and Sundays from 9 A.M. to 11 A.M. and from 4 to 6 P.M. I started at minimum wage, $4.75 an hour, but by the time I left, I was making $6.50 an hour. You don't work at an animal hospital because you want to 'get rich,' though," notes Keith. "You do it because you really care about animals.

"Also, I wanted to see what veterinary medicine was really like, I wanted to make sure it was the right career for me," he adds. (Keith will have an edge when it comes to getting into vet school; competition among applicants is fierce and vet school boards tend to favor applicants who've spent several years working at an animal hospital.)

Keith started by cleaning kennels and feeding and bathing the animals, then worked his way up to helping the doctors by restraining animals ("I had to make sure a vet didn't get bitten when he or she was examining an animal"). Keith and the other three high school students who worked at the hospital also learned how to "hold off" a vein while the doctor gave an injection or took blood, and they were encouraged to watch "surgery."

"Dr. Woltz let me watch everything from routine surgery, like neutering and spaying, to emergency operations. I was amazed by how much time and care went into prepping an animal for surgery—as well as the procedure itself. The operating room at an animal clinic looks pretty much like an O.R. in a regular hospital: The pet is hooked up to an I.V. line, there are monitors to check heart rate, etc., and the doctors and I wore masks, gloves, robes and caps. One of the most interesting operations was on a dog that had swallowed a ball; Dr. Woltz had to open up the abdomen and retrieve it. At first, it was kind of hard dealing with all the blood, but after a while I got used to it."

Keith also had to get used to "emergencies"—the dog or cat that had swallowed poison, or been hit by a car. "The office is pretty hectic when an emergency comes in," he notes. "The secretary yells, 'We have an emergency out here,' and the vets or vet technicians—or one of us students—take the animal and carry it into surgery, where it's hooked up to an I.V. line and put on a respirator if it can't breathe on its own. I stay to get the doctors whatever they need—needles or other surgical supplies. Everything has to happen very quickly."

Over time, Keith learned a great deal at the hospital, "like how to pick up on certain changes in the sick animals. You notice whether a pet isn't eating well, or seems listless, or doesn't want to go out for a walk. The vets relied on the students to alert them to any problems." Adds Keith, "I've also become much better at dealing with people. You get to know certain pets and their owners, and you learn how important it is to treat the owners as caringly as you treat their animals. I've observed how Dr. Woltz makes a point of calling clients to check on their pets after surgery, or even after something minor, like treating an eye inflammation. I've watched him calm a frightened client who's very worried about his pet—he always tries to give some positive encouragement, even in a worst-case scenario. He's helped many clients deal with a pet's serious illness or impending death. I've learned from him how to make the owners feel as though they play an important role in the pets' treatment—Dr. Woltz doesn't just take over. Instead, he explains all the options, all the available treatments. He's very patient."

Keith says that thanks to Dr. Woltz, he has an advantage in his college classes. "He taught me so much about the anatomy of animals, and the various diseases they're predisposed to, that I've already learned a lot of what's being taught in my animal science courses."

DISCOVERING WHAT *YOU* WANT TO DO

Not sure about the type of work, or career, you want to pursue after college? You can get an idea of the kind of work you'll enjoy and are suited for by making three lists. First, write down *all* your skills or talents (For example: I'm good at math; I do well in business classes; I can draw or paint; I'm great when it comes to organizing school activities.). Next, list your major interests or favorite activities (I enjoy team sports; I like to play the piano; I'm interested in anything to do with science.). Finally, make a list of the *types* of businesses you'd like to work for, or the work style you prefer (I prefer to work alone, at my own speed, with few interruptions; I enjoy a hectic fast-paced place where things happen quickly; I want a job where I can interact with other people on a daily basis; I think I'd enjoy selling things; I want to *help* people in some way.).

Once you've completed your lists, go over them carefully. You should see a pattern emerging. For example, one guy—we'll call

him "Mike"—listed "Playing clarinet in local jazz band" as one of his *talents.* Under *interests* he wrote "Listening to CDs," "Going to concerts," "Watching MTV," and "Getting together with a group of friends on weekends." Under *types of businesses and work style,* he noted that he'd "Like to work in the music field," and "I want to interact with other employees as well as the public."

Based on his lists, Mike has decided he definitely wants a career in the music or entertainment industry. To get some related experience, he's applied for an afterschool job at local record stores, shops that sell musical instruments, and for a job as an assistant in an entertainment attorney's office.

Once *you've* made a list of all the businesses in your area that could benefit from your talents, you'll be ready—or *almost* ready—to start your job search. But first take time to look over

Chapter 3, where you'll find important info on "managing your mindset"—making sure you have the positive attitude and high self-esteem necessary for tracking down and getting a great job!

3

Taking Control of Your Life

If you feel "in control" of your life—if you're basically happy with who you are, how you look, the way you interact with other people—then you've won half the battle when it comes to finding and succeeding at a job or starting your own business.

"How you feel about yourself is projected on the outside to others," says Rickell Fisher. "And before you can serve other people, whether you're working for a company *or* selling your own services or product, you need to project a positive attitude about yourself and what you're doing." Adds Rickell, "In the first 90 seconds after you meet someone, that person will form an opinion about you. You've got about a minute and a half to send them a positive message about yourself—and it's most important to remember that during a *job interview.*"

But what if you've always been a little shy, or you're nervous when it comes to going after a job, or you're afraid to start your own business because there's always the chance you might fail.

"The only thing we have to fear is fear itself." So said President Franklin Delano Roosevelt, and thousands of successful business people will tell you he was absolutely right. Once you confront the thing you fear, you have power over it—and self-confidence is born.

MAINTAIN A WINNING EDGE

"I think I have a pretty good sense of self-esteem. I don't drink. I don't mess with drugs. I'm in good physical shape because I work out. I have a healthy lifestyle.

"And, I've learned not to give up when I get discouraged. My parents always gave me a lot of support and encouraged me to keep trying—even when I didn't think I was good enough at something. In high school, there were a lot of times I felt I couldn't measure up to many of the guys on the varsity basketball team. God gave some of them incredible physical strength and talent. *I* had to spend hours and hours practicing just to catch up to them, but I made the varsity team—and now I play varsity ball in college. I used that experience to motivate myself in making my lawn service business successful—and I try to keep a positive attitude in everything I do.

"If you *think* you can't do something, if you get discouraged every time a door is slammed in your face, you'll never succeed at anything. But if you keep on trying, if you believe in yourself and persevere, you can accomplish *anything*."

—Oren Jenkins

TAMING YOUR INTERNAL CRITIC

We all have one. That little voice, that devious demon who says, "You can't do it! You'll never get that job. You don't have the experience or the talent. Start your own business? What? Are you crazy? Where will you get the time? The money? Forget it!"

That voice is our "internal critic," a nasty little pest who tries to undermine our best ideas, our hopes and dreams. And he doesn't stop there. He's constantly criticizing the way we look: "Oh, your hair will *never* be thick and gorgeous like Mary's," or "Hey, you

98-pound weakling, nobody would ever believe *you* could run your own company, that *you* could be the *boss!*" This critic gets in his digs about how other people see us, too: "Give a speech to the whole student body? You'll forget what you were going to say. You'll squeak instead of talk. All the kids will laugh at you for weeks!"

Yes, your internal critic is a busy guy, constantly bombarding you with all sorts of negative messages—and most of the time, you aren't even aware that he's shooting off his mouth. But it's

important to *become* aware of his presence—then undermine *him* before he can cut *you* down. Here's how:

Learn to recognize your critic. Whenever you start thinking *negatively* about yourself, your talents or your appearance, *your critic is at work.*

Never argue with your critic. He'll only present all sorts of new "evidence" for why a) you can't do something, b) you don't look good, or c) you will make a fool of yourself. As soon as you hear his wretched little voice, cut him off and redirect your attention. Focus on whatever you were doing before he interrupted, or take time out and go for a run, shoot some hoops, or call a friend and talk about something concerning him or her.

Your critic knows you're easy prey because you *half* believe the garbage he's spewing forth. You buy into it. And, if you've held certain beliefs ("I'm not pretty enough," or "I'll never be a good quarterback") for a long time, those thoughts are *deeply embedded in your subconscious mind* and they'll be pretty hard to root out. The best way to get rid of long-held negative beliefs is to *replace* them with positive ones.

Start by making a list of all the things you like about yourself. Write down *everything* you can think of. Here's a list one 15-year-old put together:

- I'm a pretty fair pianist and my friends ask me to play at parties.
- I do well in English and my teacher says I have potential as a writer.
- I'm good at organizing—I worked with another student to set up a food pantry for the homeless in our community.
- I'm a good actress—I just got a major part in the school play.
- I have good, close friends I can count on.

- I'm in good shape, thanks to being on the track team this year. I have shiny brown hair and pretty blue eyes. And people say my smile is really nice.

This teen's list could go on and on. If you spend an hour or two really examining yourself and your life, you're bound to discover you have many talents and attributes you'd hadn't thought of before.

Now transfer your list to a 3 *"* × 5 *"* index card. Write down all your talents and accomplishments (include awards) on the front of the card. On the back, list all the things you—or others—like about the way you look.

You've just made a "win list," a valuable card you can tuck in your wallet or purse or desk and check out every day to remind yourself (and your *critic*) of how special you are.

BOOST YOUR CONFIDENCE QUOTIENT

Want to learn more about building—and maintaining—a healthy self-image? The Corporation for Public Broadcasting has put together a smart, user-friendly booklet called "Celebrate Yourself: Six Steps to Building Your Self-Esteem."

The booklet begins with Oscar-winner Kevin Costner describing how he was a loner as a kid, a small, gangly boy with big feet—a real "late bloomer." Costner goes on to say he wished he were smarter and more disciplined. (Yes, all this from the guy who had the courage and perseverance to produce, direct, and star in the phenomenally successful *Dances With Wolves*—despite Hollywood's certainty that he couldn't pull it off.)

The booklet then gives six tried-and-true techniques for upping your confidence.

To order, send $2 (for each booklet) to CPB-Self Esteem, Box 4205, Arlington, VA 22204.

Here are some more tips for outwitting your critic:

Practice imaging—or visualizing—success. (Your critic will *hate* you for this!) Imaging, or seeing yourself as succeeding at something—whether it's making a speech to the student body or making a presentation to a potential client for your new business—is a powerful tool that Olympic and pro athletes use constantly to psych themselves up for a win. Slalom skiers and divers use imaging techniques to prepare for competition. For example, a skier fantasizes about winning *in advance;* he sees himself making a perfect run down the slope, superbly negotiating all the curves.

Practice visualizing success several times a day. Do it in the shower, on your way home from school, and most important, as you fall asleep because the mind is most receptive just before you doze off.

Practice setting goals. (This will make your critic mad—he's worked hard to discourage you from goal-setting and risk-taking.) Start with a small goal, a minor "risk" you're 90 percent sure you can succeed at. Five out of 10 people avoid setting goals because they're afraid they'll feel bad if they don't reach them. When you reach a goal, set a new one. You'll find yourself striving to meet larger, more difficult challenges—and enjoying your success.

Acquire a sense of control by doing your homework. Be aware of all the outside forces that play into the goal you're trying to reach. If you're applying for a job, try to find out as much as you can about the company. (We'll talk about "researching a company" in chapter 6). If you're starting a small business, know who your competitors are, how much your start-up costs will be, who your market is and so on. Developing a well-researched plan will give you more confidence and enthusiasm about your goal, job search, or new business.

Surround yourself with upbeat friends. Success and optimism are contagious. So are pessimism and failure. If you constantly associate with people who are negative or have a "loser" attitude, you're only giving your critic the ammunition he needs to control your thoughts.

Look good to feel good. Being well-dressed and well-groomed helps boost your self-confidence—and the confidence others have in you. But before thinking about the image you'll project on an interview there are things you must consider, which we cover in the next two chapters: the job hunt.

4

The Job Hunt, Part I: Where to Look, When to Apply, And How to Write a Résumé

You'll face some stiff competition when you look for an after-school or summer job. If you're searching for summer work, START EARLY, advises 19-year-old Jennifer Mullen, a college junior who works weekends at Pizza Hut during the school year, and weekdays and weekends during the summer.

"Most kids make the mistake of waiting until the end of May to look for a job," she explains. "But by then, all the good ones are taken. Start your job hunt in April, at the very latest. That way, you'll have your application in before the rest of the crowd."

Jennifer got her job "through a friend at college. That's a good way to get work—making a contact who can help you get the job you want. This guy worked for a Pizza Hut in our area, and he advised me to come in and fill out an application on a day when *he* was working. Then, he made sure the manager interviewed me that day so my application didn't sit on his desk for weeks."

Networking—making job contacts—is a smart idea. Tell *everybody* you know, friends, relatives, acquaintances, people at your church or temple, that you're in the market for a job and what type of work you'd like to do. If you talk to enough people, chances are someone will be able to introduce you to a person who's in a position to hire you.

A casual comment about her need for a job got one girl an internship at a magazine. She was visiting her father at his office when she ran into one of his friends on the elevator. He asked how she was doing, and she replied that she'd spent the last month looking for a summer job—preferably at a magazine or newspaper, since she planned to become a journalist—but with no luck. The friend mentioned that he knew the managing editor of a magazine for teenagers and volunteered to give the editor a call. Two weeks later, the girl received a call from a personnel rep at the magazine, and a month later, she started her summer internship—all because of a chance conversation in an elevator!

CHECKING THE WANT ADS, POUNDING THE PAVEMENT

Most of the jobs listed in the "classified" or "help wanted" section of your local and metropolitan newspapers will be aimed at adults—college grads or people with experience in a certain field. But *some* jobs can be filled by teens: part-time receptionist work, for example. These days, many working moms are opting for flex-time or job-sharing; they work during school hours, from 9 A.M. to 3 P.M., then turn over their clerical duties to a high school student who handles the 3-to-5:30 P.M. workload. To find such jobs, look for the words "part-time" or "flex-time" in ads.

Many department stores run ads for "seasonal" help to handle the holiday crunch. Check the classifieds from late October through late November if you're looking for a sales clerk or cashier job at a store. If you *do* "work Christmas"—the two to three weeks before the New Year—you'll also have a good chance at landing a *summer* job at the store.

Most teens find jobs by going "door-to-door." Just walk around

your community and look for "help wanted" or "waitress needed" signs in windows, then go in and ask to meet with the owner or manager. Stop by five or six fast-food restaurants and ask to fill out applications. Even if a business doesn't have a "help-wanted" sign in the window, walk in anyway and ask the receptionist for an application—you never know what may come up in the future.

If you're applying for a job at a big corporation, manufacturing plant, or major department store, go directly to the personnel or human resources department and fill out an application form. Although *most* major companies will call you back for an interview at a later date, do be prepared to interview the same day you fill out the application—recruiters occasionally have a free moment and will see "walk-ins". Make sure you're wearing "interview clothes."

Don't forget to check out summer jobs at amusement parks, the local Y (many sponsor day camps and need counselors), area repair shops (if you have a knack for fixing things), jewelry stores—any organization or business that *might* have an opening.

Expect your job hunt to take at least two months (though some lucky teens find jobs within the first week, possibly because they're at the right place at the right time).

YOUR RÉSUMÉ—IT'S YOUR CALLING CARD

Whatever job you're going after, it's a good idea to have a résumé. Most kids *won't* have one—so a professional-looking résumé can help you stand out from the crowd. You can also send a résumé, along with a cover letter, to corporations and small businesses to inquire about *possible* job opportunities; ask to meet with someone in personnel to talk about job openings that might occur in the *future.* Or you *could* call the company's executive offices, ask for the name of the president, and write directly to him or her. If you write a persuasive, intelligent letter detailing your strengths, talents and interests, and explaining why you want to work for that particular company, the person at the top (or that person's secretary or assistant) will most likely send your letter on to personnel. A letter that's forwarded from the "president's office" has a good chance of getting noticed, so you may receive a call from a personnel rep asking you to come in for an "exploratory" interview.

You should also take a copy of your résumé to a job interview. By handing the interviewer a résumé, you provide him with tangible proof of your talents and skills.

But how can you write a résumé when you haven't got any *work experience?* It's actually very easy.

"I didn't have a résumé when I applied for my first job—but I realize now I could easily have written one listing all my volunteer experience and high school activities. Many times, kids think a résumé has to list *formal* job experience. But actually, a good résumé just has to give the employer an idea of your skills and talents. I didn't know it at the time, but I had a résumé all written—in my head."

—*Rickell Fisher*

Using the workspace below, write down your educational background. Start with high school and work backward to grade school, noting the dates you attended each. Then, list "work" experience, such as babysitting, clerking at your mom's florist shop, caddying for a few of your dad's friends, running errands for people in the neighborhood. Next, jot down every volunteer "job" you've ever held—anything from mowing your elderly neighbor's lawn to serving meals at a homeless shelter. Finally, list your accomplishments and any awards you've received, plus school and community activities you're involved in.

_____

_____

_____

_____

_____

_____

_____

_____

Now, take a look at the sample résumé below. Following this format, use what you've recorded in the workspace to put together *your* résumé.

If you have access to a computer, you can play around with the form at, printing section headings and your name in boldface type for emphasis. You can also use a computer to run off 40 or 50 copies, or pay a résumé service to produce 50 to 100 copies. A résumé service will give you the option of using different typefaces for a truly professional look. Expect to pay $50 to $60 for their work.

SAMPLE RÉSUMÉ

Karen Clark
1212 West Birch Street
Seattle, Washington 98166
(206) 555-1212

EDUCATION
West Seattle High School, September 1990-present
Eastlake Middle School, September 1987-June 1990
Montrose Elementary School, September 1981-June 1987
High School Grade-Point Average: 3.6 (out of 4.0)

WORK EXPERIENCE
Mother's helper, 1989-present. Take care of seven-year-old girl from 3 p.m. to 6 p.m., Monday through Friday, and from 8 a.m. to 1 p.m., Saturdays. Do light housekeeping and laundry for the child's mother.

VOLUNTEER EXPERIENCE
Highlands Community Hospital, Pediatric Department, Seattle, Washington. Nurse's assistant, summer 1990.
Delivered meal trays to patients, helped make patients comfortable, ran errands for five nurses, did light typing and clerical

work. Meals-On-Wheels, Burien, Washington. Transporter, summer 1991. Delivered hot meals to homebound elderly.

SCHOOL ACTIVITIES
Assistant director, 1991 West Seattle High School musical, "Grease." President, Future Nurses of America, 1990-present. Junior Class treasurer, 1991.

REFERENCES ON REQUEST

BEEF UP YOUR RÉSUMÉ . . .
. . . and get valuable on-the-job experience (while helping others) by becoming a volunteer. Below is a sampling of organizations that need volunteer workers:

Nursing homes and adult day-care centers
Hospitals
Homeless shelters and soup kitchens
Animal shelters
Local libraries
Lighthouse (for the Blind)
Meals-on-Wheels programs
Food collection agencies
Food pantries
Crisis hotlines
Community centers
Environmental groups
Political campaigns
Recycling centers
The Salvation Army
The Red Cross
United Way
YMCA/YWCA
Zoos
Pet visitor programs (transporting shelter animals to homes)

COVER YOURSELF

Whether you're answering an ad in the classifieds, applying for a job you've *heard* is available, or writing about possible *future* openings at a particular organization, always attach a "cover letter" to your résumé. A cover letter will personalize your résumé, and tell the recruiter or boss or company owner that you've taken the time to sit down and think about the job (or company), and are serious about finding work. When possible, avoid addressing letters to "Dear Sir" or "Dear Madam," or "To Whomever It May Concern." Call the company and get a name—even if it's the name of the director of personnel or human resources. If you're answering a newspaper ad that lists a box number only, "Dear Sir or Madam" is fine.

Here's a sample letter from a teen who's inquiring about possible openings at an animal hospital:

1251 Grover Street
Yonkers, NY 10707
January 20, 1992

Dr. Carol Kelsey
All Creatures Great and Small
   Animal Hospital
351 Ardsley Road
Scarsdale, NY 10607

Dear Dr. Kelsey,

I'm writing to you about possible afterschool work as a kennel attendant at your hospital.

You may remember me. My family brought our cat, Barney, to your hospital for most of his life. I often accompanied my mother or father when they took Barney in for his shots or treatments, since I've always had a keen interest in animals. You very kindly let me listen to Barney's heart through your stethoscope, and you answered all my "little kid" questions with great patience.

As you can see by the enclosed résumé, I'm now a sophomore in high school, and I'm planning to major in animal science in college. I'd very much like to become a veterinarian and feel I could learn a great deal by working with you.

I realize you may not have any job openings at present, but I'd really appreciate it if you could take time to meet with me to discuss possible future openings at the hospital. I will call you after 3 P.M. one day next week.

Thanks so much for your consideration. I look forward to hearing from you.

Sincerely,

Kim Lee

Here's a letter a teen has written about a specific job opening:

875 Glendale Avenue
Escondido, CA 10028
March 15, 1992

Mr. Ray McMahon
Personnel Director
ACE Industries
1010 Wayland Drive
San Diego, CA 10027

Dear Mr. McMahon,

I'm writing in response to your recent advertisement for part-time workers that appeared in the *San Diego Gazette.*

I understand your company is looking for young people to work as messengers, "gofers," and clerical help. As you can see by the enclosed résumé, I have considerable experience operating both computers and word processors (I also type 75 wpm). Although I'm interested in any position with ACE, I feel my background has best prepared me for work in one of your clerical departments.

Thank you so much for your time and consideration. I will call you in the near future.

Sincerely,

James Martin

If you've checked out all the advice in this chapter, you've completed "step 1" in your job search—and you're ready for step 2: creating the right image. It's about putting together a winning look for your job search and interview.

5

The Job Hunt, Part II: Creating the Right Image

"He's well-packaged." That's a term commonly used in Corporate America. Sometimes, you'll hear an employee comment that a colleague or boss is "well-packaged." Often, an interviewer or corporate recruiter will use the phrase to describe a job applicant. Being well-packaged simply means giving others the impression that you have it all together—at least *outwardly*. The well-packaged job applicant has a confident (but not *overly* confident) manner, maintains eye contact with the interviewer, is relaxed, smiles—and last, but certainly not least, has a pulled-together look that comes from being impeccably groomed and appropriately dressed.

CLOTHES ENCOUNTERS

Pick your interview outfit carefully. It may not seem fair, but the person who interviews you will make certain judgments based on what you're wearing. And, remember that the *type* of business and job should determine the kind of outfit you choose.

Linda Tyson, Human Resources Manager for Avon Products, Inc., advises that applicants aim for a neat, conservative look when interviewing at a corporation or medium to small office. "Avoid trendy clothes, tee shirts, and loud, garishly colored items.

If you're applying for an office job, you don't need to go out and buy an 'interview suit.' Most teens will be able to find an appropriate interview outfit in their closets. Girls can choose a dress and jacket combination, or a blouse or sweater and skirt duo. For guys, a long-sleeved pin stripe or solid color shirt, tie and dark slacks are fine. A sport coat will add to the look but isn't absolutely necessary. Above all, make sure your clothes are clean and neatly pressed.''

Dr. Michael Woltz, a Scarsdale, New York, veterinarian says "When kids come in too 'decked out,' wearing a suit or an expensive dress, I can't help feeling they won't be happy working at an animal hospital, scrubbing cages, getting their hands dirty. Maybe I'm making an unfair assessment, but I've found that the more casually dressed applicants end up fitting in better." Noting that his student employees wear "scrubs" (hospital attire) over jeans and sweats when they're on the job, Woltz gives a thumbs up to slacks and sweater (or shirt) combinations for both guys and girls. Even clean, neatly pressed jeans and a clean tee get passing marks.

So, how do you decide what type of outfit will impress your future employer? Dressy and polished? Or casual and comfortable? Here's a quick, 99 percent foolproof guide.

If you're interviewing for a job at a major corporation or small office or business, wear:

Guys
- A sport coat, conservative shirt, tie, dark slacks
- A long-sleeved, conservative shirt and tie and dark slacks
Girls
- A conservative, tailored dress (avoid loud prints or "little girl" flowers), topped with a jacket
- A long-sleeved blouse and knee-length skirt
- A nice, long-sleeved jewel-necked sweater and skirt

If you're applying for a job at a bank, law office, or any other super-conservative type of business, opt for:

Guys
- A gray, navy or pin stripe suit with conservative shirt and tie
- A navy jacket, slate gray slacks, solid color or narrow pin stripe shirt and tie

Girls
- A jacket and dress combination
- A jacket and skirt duo, or an unstructured suit

If you're applying for a job at a trendy boutique, department store, specialty shop, yogurt or ice cream shop, or a position in one of the "creative" fields (advertising, publishing, graphic design), wear:

Guys
- A sport coat, shirt, tie and slacks
- A long-sleeved shirt, tie and slacks
- A shirt, tie, pullover sweater and slacks

Girls
- A skirt and sweater or skirt and blouse combination (you can get away with brighter colors if you're interviewing at a boutique or graphic design firm)
- A long, stylish jacket and tailored slacks
- A sweater that looks like a jacket, plus tailored slacks, or a skirt that's about 1 inch above the knee
- A one- or two-piece wool or cotton-knit dress

If you're applying for a job at a fast-food restaurant (or any other kind of restaurant), wear:

Guys
- A long-sleeved shirt (in the summer, short-sleeved is fine) and slacks, a sweater and slacks, or a sport coat and slacks. A tie is a good bet.

Girls
- A stylish jacket and tailored slacks or skirt
- A sweater (or blouse) and skirt
- A dress

If you're applying for work in a very casual, hands-on setting, such as an animal hospital, kennel, construction firm, lawn service, housepainting business, opt for:

Guys
- Shirt and slacks or sweater and slacks (tie is optional)

Girls
- A blouse or sweater teamed with slacks or a skirt

(In some cases, both guys and girls can get away with clean, neat jeans and a sweater or brand-new tee—check with other employees to see what *they* wore on their interviews.)

> "When I applied for a summer job at a big advertising agency, my mom 'styled' my outfit for the interview. She knew the people at the agency—and was aware that I could wear slacks instead of a dress or skirt. We chose a long, tailored jacket and slacks, both in washed silk. It was a polished, but comfortable, look. I didn't feel under- or over-dressed."
>
> *—Kate Cusick,*
> a teenager from New York

WHAT NOT TO WEAR ON AN INTERVIEW

There are some definite *don'ts* when it comes to interview outfits. Here's what to avoid:

Girls

- The too-short skirt (that you have to keep pulling down when you're seated). Ideally, your skirt should be knee-length or longer, or an inch (at most) above your knees.
- Tight pants, snug skirts, skimpy sweater, "Spandex" anything.
- Sandals, open-toed or sling-back shoes—or shoes with spiky heels (flats or low-heeled pumps are smart choices).
- Wildly-patterned leggings or stockings. Choose nude or flesh-toned stockings—and never go bare-legged to an interview.
- Jeans and tees (unless you're applying for one of those "special" jobs we mentioned).
- Flashy accessories, such as dangling earrings, over-sized hair ornaments—and jangling bracelets (a common "interview disaster" according to recruiters who say clanking bracelets draw their attention away from what you're saying). Keep accessories simple and choose classic

pieces: button, or gold coin, or pearl earrings, or small gold hoops; a wide silver or gold cuff; a gold, silver or dark metal pin; a simple rope of "pearls," or gold or silver beads.

Kathleen Walas, author and International Beauty and Fashion Director for Avon, advises that you make sure your accessories are properly balanced. "Jewelry placement involves four primary focal points: the ears, neck, shoulders and wrist. Too much or too little in any one area looks awkward or 'unfinished.' If you wear a pin on the left shoulder, try a bracelet on the right wrist, or vice versa. When you wear a necklace *and* a pin, each should be simple. The necklace should be long to avoid clutter at the throat area. Earrings should provide a finished, balanced look. If you wear big, somewhat bold earrings, keep other accessories on the small side. If you choose a more dramatic pin or necklace, opt for smaller earrings."

Guys
- Gold necklaces, earrings, bracelets. "Remove or put your jewelry inside your shirt," advises Linda Tyson. "Earrings should be removed before an interview—most employers go for a conservative look."
- Sneakers (or any athletic-style shoes), deck shoes. Wear loafers or lace-up shoes.
- Jackets with the sleeves rolled up (unless you're applying for a job at a "creative" business where bosses and employees dress in casual or trendy clothing).
- Short-sleeved shirts or polos (unless you've been told by current employees that this attire is acceptable).
- Jeans and tees (unless you're going after one of the specialty jobs we've talked about).

DETAILS MAKE THE DIFFERENCE

Make sure your shoes are shined and in good shape. Have last year's shoes re-soled and the heels replaced. Polish until scuff marks disappear. If you carry a purse, tote, briefcase or attaché to the interview, make certain it's in good condition. Touch up scuff marks on vinyl or leather carry-alls with polish or a permanent ink felt-tip pen in a matching color. (Felt-tips work well in touching up toe scuffs too!)

—*Kathleen Walas,*
author of *Real Beauty . . . Real Women*

GOOD GROOMING MAKES GOOD SENSE

When you're putting together your interview outfit, don't forget the rest of the package—*you!* Your hair, makeup, nails—all play into your *image*. Interviewers notice *everything* about job applicants. One corporate recruiter tells about the time she interviewed a potential summer employee—and forgot most of what he said because his hair kept flopping into his eyes. "Every time he raised his hand to push his hair back—which happened about once a minute—I'd lose my train of thought!" she recalls. "He didn't get the job, which was working as an office administrator. I figured if he couldn't control his hair, he couldn't keep track of all the jobs we'd have him doing."

HAIR STRATEGIES

"Make sure your hair is neat, clean and conservatively styled," advises Linda Tyson. "Avoid 'trendy' styles, big pouffy or wildly curly, uncontrollable hair." Tyson suggests girls opt for slightly off-the-face styles. If you have long hair, use a headband to pull it back, or secure it at the nape of your neck with a barrette to make it look neat. Does your hair tend to have a mind of its own? Lightly mist with hairspray so it'll stay put during the interview.

Guys should choose a fairly short style, according to Tyson. The front should be cut so that it doesn't flop into your eyes. And, avoid styles with long hair on top or at the nape of the neck.

DON'T MAKE THESE MAKEUP MISTAKES
Girls need to pay special attention to makeup. Not wearing makeup will give you that "little girl" look—just what you want to avoid when interviewing for a job. Too much makeup can make you look tough. Aim for a natural, subtle look: Use a water-based foundation (match to skin tone *exactly* by testing on your jaw) and blend well around the edges so there's no telltale line. If you're prone to oily skin and breakouts, pat concealer one shade lighter than your skin tone onto any blemishes, then dust loose powder lightly over your foundation and concealer to "set." Use a cotton ball to buff away excess. Apply a neutral shade of blush to the "apples" of your cheeks (to find the apples, smile— they're the round, fleshy area). Don't "over-blush." Your aim is a healthy glow.

Choose neutral eye makeup and lip colors. Opt for brown, gray, taupe, muted plum, or mauve shadow—and use just a hint on the lid. Mist a toothbrush with hairspray and comb upward through brows to shape and tame. Apply one or two coats of brown or brown/black mascara on upper lashes only. Use a lash comb to remove mascara clumps, and press a tissue gently against lashes to "blot" excess color and prevent "raccoon eyes." (Be sure to use waterproof, smudge-proof mascara.) A natural stain of lip color will complete your look.

If your skin gets greasy quickly, carry facial blotting tissues in your purse and pat over forehead, nose and chin just before you get to the interview site.

SENSIBLE SCENTS

If you use fragrance, choose a scent that's subtle—not over-powering. Mist *lightly* onto insides of elbows, wrists, or spray onto a dressy hanky you tuck into your blazer pocket.

Guys, go easy on the aftershave and cologne.

—*Kathleen Walas*

HANDS-ON HOW-TOS

A manicure is a must for both girls and guys. (Yes, guys, top male Wall Street execs and corporate presidents get weekly professional manicures.) It's not a bad idea to invest $5 or $10 in a professional manicure prior to your first interview. After that, you can do your own weekly manicure. Start by soaking fingertips (nails should be polish-free, girls) in warm, soapy water for five minutes to soften rough cuticles (if they're very rough and tough, add a capful of baby oil to the water). Use one end of an orange stick to gently clean under nail tips. Then, wrap the other end in cotton, dip into olive oil, and use to gently push back cuticles. Use a cuticle clipper to snip away hangnails. (Guys, if you *don't* use an orange stick to tame cuticles, keep them in check with this easy trick: every A.M., while showering, use the edge of a clean, damp washcloth to gently push them back.)

To keep cuticles neat, massage with a rich hand lotion after showering and before bedtime.

Girls, opt for short, neatly filed nails (file in a slightly oval or square shape for a professional look—and make sure nail tips don't extend more than ⅛ inch beyond your fingertips). Pack away your bright or frosted polishes; instead, choose a subtle creme formula in colors such as buff, nude, pale peach, or soft rose. One of the best interview (and on-the-job) nail looks: the

French manicure. Start by stroking basecoat onto nail. Then brush a creamy white or neutral beige enamel onto tip only (stroke brush across tip, following natural line of nail, in one smooth sweep). Apply sheer pink or clear enamel over the entire nail (use two coats for a more protective, glossier finish).

Your manicure should look super-neat. To remove polish smudges from cuticles, dip an orange stick into polish remover and wipe lightly over smudge. Touch up a "nick" or chipped polish by applying a tiny bit of enamel to chipped area only. Allow to dry. Then smooth a coat of polish over the entire nail, and finish with topcoat. (In a super rush? Quick-dry polish by dipping your finger into ice water for 20 seconds.)

BREATHING LESSONS

Of course, you'll brush and floss your teeth scrupulously and use mouthwash before your interview. But to be absolutely sure your breath is fresh, carry breath spray in your purse or pocket and use it just before you enter the building.

—Kathleen Walas

Okay. You've scoped out the job market, written your résumé, and polished your image. Now it's time to prepare for the *interview*. For a guide to "smart interviewing," check out the next chapter.

6

The Job Hunt, Part III: The Interview

It's finally happened. After weeks (or months) of sending out résumés, filling out applications, and going door-to-door to inquire about job openings, an employer has actually called you for AN INTERVIEW.

DO YOUR HOMEWORK

You've chosen your interview outfit, invested in a new haircut and a manicure—so what's left? Plenty!

First, you need to "research the company." "You'll want to know as much as possible about the business you're interviewing at," says Linda Menzies. "By knowing the company, you'll be able to ask informed questions and make intelligent statements about the business—and that will tell the interviewer you took the time to research the organization and that you know something about the type of work you'll be doing."

If you're applying for a job at a large corporation, call the main office and ask for a copy of the annual report, which will give you a good idea about the corporation's holdings, its profits for a given year, and the type of product or service it provides. If the company isn't able to send you an annual report, do some checking at your local library. The reference librarian can direct you to books and reports, such as *Dun & Bradstreet's Reference of Corporate Managements* or *Standard & Poor's,* that give info on major corporations. You can also do some "generic" reading. For example, if you want to work for an organization like Boeing, check out books and articles focusing on the aerospace industry.

SPEAK UP!

It's normal to get the "pre-interview" jitters. But remember, the more you go through the interview process, the better you'll become at fielding tough questions.

You *can* curb your nervousness by *rehearsing,* Linda Menzies advises. "Whenever I interview for a job, I make a 'mental outline,' organizing my thoughts, thinking about what I want to say, and anticipating specific questions—and my responses. I practice in front of a mirror, checking to see if I'm smiling, using my hands too much, etc. By rehearsing, you'll feel more prepared, more comfortable and in control.

"A lot of young people—me included—tend to punctuate our speech with 'ummmms' and 'you knows' and 'likes.' As you rehearse, try to edit these out of your vocabulary."

Honesty is the best policy when you get into an interview, Linda says. "During one interview, I was so nervous I started to stutter. Instead of trying to pretend I was in control (which I obviously *wasn't*), I admitted to the interviewer that I was a little nervous. He immediately became more relaxed and much nicer when asking the questions. It was as though he *wanted* me to do well. I got the job."

Linda also suggests you take advantage of junior high and high school resources, such as a guidance counselor, to help you become a more confident interviewee. "Public speaking classes, debate, radio and TV production (if they're offered)—all can help you think clearly, organize your thoughts, and speak intelligently."

—Linda Menzies

Applying to a small business? It won't have an annual report, but your local Chamber of Commerce can give you some specifics about the product or service the company provides. You can also call or visit the business beforehand. "My mom owns a florist shop," says Linda Menzies, "and if I were a teen applying to work for her, I'd stop by the shop, or call, to find out what kinds of flowers she sells—whether she specializes in live or artificial flowers—or if she also sells specialty items, like planters, wreaths, arts and craft products. That way, I'd have a basic knowledge of the business before I was in an interview situation."

NINE STRATEGIES FOR SMART INTERVIEWING

Linda Tyson, Human Resources Manager for Avon Products, Inc., offers these tips for a successful interview:

1. Be on time. Plan to arrive five, 10—even 20—minutes early. If someone's late for an interview, it gives the impression he or she may not be dependable, or may not be that interested in finding a job.

2. If you haven't already filled out an application, and are asked to do so right before the interview, *take your time.* Make sure your handwriting is legible, and that words are correctly spelled. Take a few minutes to think about the questions so you give the best answers. If the application is sloppy, it may reflect on the job applicant's work style. If you don't understand something, leave that space blank—or ask the receptionist or the person who gave you the application for clarification.

3. Use a firm handshake—but don't "break" the interviewer's hand. If the interviewer comes out of the office to meet you, stand up and shake the interviewer's hand. Pick up your coat, tote or briefcase immediately afterward.

4. Once you're in the interviewer's office, sit up straight; you want to project the impression that you're poised. Don't lean

over the desk or sit slumped in your chair with your legs stretched out in front of you. And avoid folding your arms across your chest.

5. If you can indicate an interest in a specific job, that's great (many corporations have a space on applications where you can list the position desired). Be prepared to tell why you think you're qualified to fill a particular slot. Rather than giving yes or no answers, elaborate somewhat, pointing out your strong points. If you're applying for a clerical job, for example, emphasize your organizational skills, typing, word processing or computer experience.

6. Be enthusiastic, but don't go off on a tangent. Listen very carefully to the question, and focus on answering it. It's remarkable how many people don't answer the question that's been asked. For some interviewers, this indicates lack of concentration or poor listening skills.

7. Tell the interviewer about any previous work experience—babysitting jobs, working at a fast-food restaurant, helping out at your parents' business, volunteering. Then, tell what you learned from that experience: dependability, interpersonal skills, sales skills, budgeting, etc.

8. Don't bring up money at the beginning of the interview. Allow the interviewer to talk about salary (in *rare* cases, he or she may ask what type of salary *you're* looking for, so it's wise to have talked with other teens in similar jobs to find out what they're making). If the interviewer offers you a job then and there—but hasn't mentioned salary—you can ask what the job pays. (Some interviewers will call you back for a second interview, or make a phone offer at a later date and talk about salary then.

9. At the end of the interview, shake the interviewer's hand and thank him or her for meeting with you. The next day, send a typed thank you note to the interviewer, emphasizing your interest in the job and the company. If you haven't heard from

a prospective employer two weeks after the interview, call and ask if the job has been filled, or if you're still under consideration. If the position *has* been offered to someone else, be sure to ask the interviewer to keep you in mind for any other positions within the company.

QUESTIONS THAT MAY CROP UP
DURING AN INTERVIEW

1. Tell me about yourself. ("This is the hardest to answer," says Linda Menzies. "You want to emphasize your talents and strengths *without* sounding like a prima donna. Rehearse what you plan to say before the interview. PS: Don't volunteer a lot of irrelevant "personal" info.)

2. What kind of job are you looking for? Or: Why do you think you'd be a good fit for this particular position?

3. Do you know anything about our company?

4. What are your major strengths?

5. What are your weaknesses? (Applicants usually stumble over this one. Mention a "minor" weakness—one that actually has a positive aspect—such as, "I'm very enthusiastic about whatever project I take on, sometimes to the point of being a perfectionist. I'm learning to do the best I can [on a school project, for example], then to move on to the next task at hand.")

6. What activities are you involved in at school? In the community?

7. Do you have any work experience? (This is when you bring up the babysitting job, volunteer work, helping "Uncle Mack" at his hardware store, etc.)

8. How do you think your experience will help you in this job?

9. What do you plan to major in when you go to college? What do you want to do after college?

—*Linda Menzies*

THE FOLLOW-UP NOTE

By writing a post-interview thank you note, you let the interviewer know you're seriously interested in the job, and that you appreciated the time he took to meet with you. You'll also rekindle his memory—and that may be all it takes to win a job if you're neck and neck with another equally qualified applicant.

Here's a sample thank you:

Dear Ms. Gleason,

I'd like to thank you for taking time from your busy schedule to meet with me regarding the clerking job at Gleason Florists.

I enjoyed talking with you and learning more about the florist business, and I'd very much like to spend my summer working for you. As I mentioned when we met, I'm an avid gardener and think my knowledge of flowers would help me in my work at the shop.

Again, thanks so much for meeting with me. I look forward to hearing from you.

Sincerely,

Ken Cohen

Here's another:

Dear Ms. Merchant,

Thank you for taking time from your busy schedule to interview me for Merchant Travel's summer internship program.

I enjoyed meeting with you and am very excited about the possibility of working at Merchant this summer. I've always been interested in the travel business and feel I could learn a great deal in your internship program. You mentioned that

the intern's duties include sorting and sending travel brochures to various clients, then following up by phone to make
certain they received the materials. I enjoy working with
people and would welcome the opportunity to deal directly
with Merchant's customers in this way.

Again, thank you for taking the time to talk with me. I look
forward to hearing from you soon.

Sincerely,

Michael Norris

After two, three—possibly four—interviews, it's likely you'll have
landed a job. In the next chapter, we'll tell you how to make a
success of it.

7

The Working Life (How to Succeed In Business)

It's your first day on the job, so we'll start at the beginning: what to wear. (Remind you of the first day of school? Unfortunately, in this case, there's no "best friend" to call so you can compare "first day" outfits!)

Weather permitting, you can wear what you wore for your interview—it impressed your employers once. Otherwise, a basic jacket, shirt, tie and nice slacks combo will work well for guys; for girls, a skirt and blouse (or sweater), or a jacket and dress duo are appropriate for most office situations. Depending on your gender, you'll have to wear a tie or pantyhose, no matter *how* hot it is that first day.

If you work at a fast-food restaurant or hospital, you're lucky—you'll wear a uniform. And, if you're an attendant at an animal shelter, kennel or animal hospital, we advise that you wear clean jeans and a clean tee or sweatshirt, which, of course, will be covered by the "scrubs" your boss will provide.

Before you invest in an entirely new work wardrobe, take at least a week to analyze what your officemates and superiors wear. There's no sense in spending several hundred dollars on a new suit if slacks and a shirt, plus the sport coat hanging in the back of your closet, will do just fine.

"My first day on the job at an ad agency I showed up wearing a skirt and jacket—and everyone else was wearing slacks. Some people were even wearing jeans! My boss explained that this was 'approved *summer* dress' and that I could chose my clothes accordingly."

—*Kate Cusick*

JUST THE BASICS, PLEASE . . .

Once you've figured out what the "office uniform" is, spend a weekend (or better yet, several evenings when stores are less crowded) shopping for a few basic items that will see you through the summer, or year, if you work an afterschool job. Look for quality fabrics that will last: 100 percent wool jackets, slacks and skirts are good bets for fall and winter; wool *blends* tend to "pill" and wear thin. For summer, opt for cotton or linen pieces with a *hint* of polyester, which will help the clothing hold its shape, curb wrinkling—and cut down on your ironing time.

Girls, look for "washable" or "sueded" silk slacks, dresses and jackets, polyester dresses that look like fine silk, or cotton-knit dresses, which will hold their shape in warm weather. Guys, opt for cotton/poly blend shirts and slacks, or tropical weight wool slacks. Most offices are over-heated during the winter, so choose *lightweight* jackets rather than heavier ones. In the summer, air-conditioning units are often set at full blast, so keep a jacket or cotton-knit sweater on hand.

Here's a breakdown of the basics you'll need for a typical office summer job (be sure to check your closet before shopping).

Girls:

One or two simply styled dresses ("coatdresses" are a good bet); two skirts; three blouses; one or two pairs of slacks; one or two unstructured jackets.

Guys:

Three pairs of slacks; four or five shirts; one or two sport coats (optional); one cotton knit sweater (optional); three ties.

Shop sales and outlets for bargains—but be sure to check for superior workmanship and quality. Like your mom, scrutinize every seam, look for "pulls" in sweaters, and check to see whether items are washable (dry cleaning is costly!).

ADD-ONS . . .

Once you've put together a work wardrobe, you can use accessories to create your own look. Earrings, a necklace, a sophisticated "cuff" bracelet, a pretty scarf—all can add up to great style. Keep accessories neat and discreet (unless the majority of other employees are into "trendy" pieces), and be sure to follow our smart accessorizing tips in Chapter 5.

Guys, all you'll need is a classy watch to complete your on-the-job look.

GROOMING COUNTS

Just as you paid special attention to grooming before your interview, be sure your hair, makeup and nails look terrific now that you've *got* the job. Both girls and guys should opt for fairly conservative hairstyles (be sure to keep it clean) and well-manicured hands (a weekly at-home manicure is a must). Girls, keep makeup natural and subtle.

SIZING UP THE CORPORATE CULTURE

"Corporate culture" doesn't refer to the artwork hanging on the walls or the architecture magazines on the waiting room tables. Corporate culture is, according to anthropologist Steve Barnett, Ph.D., "the rules, values and symbols that underlie and determine how corporate decisions are made and how everyday life in a company is experienced."

One good way to take your company's pulse: read its printed materials. Annual reports, if available, should give you a pretty clear idea of how the company wants outsiders to perceive it. Perhaps more important, though, are the newsletters, memos, and bulletins that land in your "in-box." Though *seemingly* informal, newsletters can help you figure out what the company expects of its employees, and how you should behave if you want to get ahead in the corporation. Remember that whatever appears in the company newsletter is there because senior management *wants* it there. A newsletter will show you who the "company heroes" are. And if the newsletter includes a "suggestion coupon" to be clipped, filled in, and sent to management, you can be *fairly* certain the company welcomes and rewards innovators and creative thinkers.

Most companies claim to value creativity. But if the "employee of the month" column is regularly devoted to those who've played it safe and toed the corporate line, that's your cue to follow your boss's directives to the letter.

If the company heroes are people who come in early, stay late, and rarely interrupt their work—even to hit the washroom or go to lunch—you know you're in a real nose-to-the-grindstone office and you're wise to behave accordingly.

There are other ways to "read" your corporation's culture. For example, take a close look at how your colleagues behave (especially the ones the boss seems to favor). Does everybody call the boss "Sylvia," or is she referred to as "Ms. Caridge"? Do people who work late get kudos from the boss—or does management follow the adage "if you can't get your work done by 5 P.M., you're doing something wrong"? Do most employees stay at their desks, or is the office more casual, with co-workers meeting at the water cooler to exchange bits of information (business and otherwise)? Or, do they stop by the boss's office to chat for a few minutes?

During your first few weeks on the job, you'll gradually discover what's acceptable and expected behavior, and what isn't. In the meantime, follow these two cardinal rules of business:

- When you start a new job, listen and learn. Don't start talking before you have something worthwhile to say.
- Be nice to *everybody*. Sometimes the least likely person has the boss's ear. And, you never know whom you'll end up socializing with, or working for—or depending on.

FINDING A MENTOR

Your teenage co-workers aren't the only "friends" you may have at the office. Often, your best friend will be someone who's not only older than you, but a person you have little in common with, except that you work for the same company. This friend is your "mentor," a boss or colleague who has, for one reason or another, decided to take you under his or her wing and show you the ropes. In fact, one of the best ways to learn the corporate ropes (and get promotions) is to learn from a pro, someone who's already succeeded in your field of interest.

> "I became friends with my supervisor, a 26-year-old woman who'd been with the company for several years. If there was something I didn't know how to do, she patiently helped me. She explained lots of things about the agency and the people I'd be working with. She made things much easier for me."
>
> —*Kate Cusick*

After you've been on the job awhile, you'll realize the office environment sparks more unanswered questions in your mind than the toughest trig course you ever faced in school. The work world can be confusing and confounding—and often there are no tutors to help you.

If you're lucky, your mentor will find you. Is there someone above you who seems to be taking an interest in your work and in seeing you succeed? Is there somebody whose style you admire and want to emulate? Is there someone who recognizes that the best way to lead is to teach, and that the best people to teach are those who are young, bright, and eager—like you? This person may make an an ideal mentor who can help you tremendously in learning new skills and picking up on workplace savvy.

"Lots of people can talk, but few can really *listen successfully*— either to their boss, a co-worker, a customer, or a mentor. If you listen objectively, putting your feelings of frustration or anger aside for a few minutes—even in a situation where your boss is criticizing you for something you've done wrong or overlooked—things you haven't understood before often start to become clear.

"Also, if you don't feel good about your job, or your work situation because your boss doesn't listen to *you*—he doesn't seem to 'hear' your ideas or merely dismisses them—ask to sit down with him when he's not busy or preoccupied and talk about how you can do your job better. Ask him if there are certain things he likes about the way you work, as well as areas you can improve. This approach will open the lines of communication between the two of you, and it'll show the boss you're really serious about doing a terrific job."

—*Rickell Fisher*

If, by your second or third week on the job, no one has "adopted" you, choose your ideal mentor. Make yourself visible to him by dint of your hard work and pleasant personality, thus inspiring him to take you under his wing. Once you've found your mentor, be willing to work hard, to observe, to learn—and to take your mentor's constructive criticism in the spirit it's meant. You can learn to handle criticism by *learning from it.* Whenever your mentor—or any superior—critiques your work, ask yourself: Will following the critic's suggestions bring me closer to a goal? If the criticism is vague, ask for more specifics. Make the giver feel comfortable—don't get defensive. If you're receptive, you'll encourage your mentor to continue giving you both negative *and* positive feedback.

WORKING SMART—AND CHEERFULLY

The first day on the job can be mind-boggling (for that matter, so can the first week!). There are a zillion things to absorb, from finding and operating the copy machine to figuring out how you're going to make time for the 101 tasks your superior is blithely tossing at you.

Most everyone—no matter how many jobs they've held— feels overwhelmed the first few days in a new position. But you can make things easier by getting organized. First, make a master list of all the projects your supervisor wants you to handle. Then, sit down with her and ask which projects take priority—and which ones can be moved to the end of the list. Get deadlines for each task, if possible. If you have any questions about how to do a particular job, ask *now* (don't try to wing it).

When tackling a big project, break it down into smaller, more manageable steps (it will help to list the steps on a piece of paper or "month-at-a-glance" calendar). Each day, plan to complete a certain number of steps. Set your deadline, then work backward from that date. Do a little each day in a logical sequence until the project is completed.

If you're prone to wasting time, break the habit—fast! Take a good look at how you spend your day. Do you rack up 15 minutes just walking back and forth between your desk and the water cooler? Then get an attractive insulated jug and fill it with ice water each morning. Or do you spend hours trying to locate mislabeled files? Come in early during the week, or ask to spend a Saturday morning at the office (when fewer people will be around to distract you) and redo your filing system.

SERVICE WITH A SMILE

It's only natural that there will be times when your job gets you down. You won't agree with your boss, or a co-worker or customer will do something that annoys you, or you'll simply have so much work to do that you'll feel irritable and tempted to snap at the first person who walks by.

But hold your tongue and rein in your emotions, say the experts; later, when you get home you can vent your frustrations to a friend or one of your parents.

"There are times when I really feel like screaming," says Jennifer Mullen, who works part-time at a fast-food restaurant. "I'd worked at an expensive, 'upscale' restaurant before taking my Pizza Hut job, and the individual tips at that other restaurant were bigger." However, the tables "turned" only once or twice a night, she adds, so her take-home pay wasn't that great.

"Pizza Hut pays me $2.90 an hour to waitress (less than minimum wage, because they know I'll make up the difference in tips). The tables turn over quickly—and on a good afternoon, I've taken home $70 in tips, *after* I've split my share with the busboy. But sometimes we get a big family or a group of guys who push four or five tables together and sit for a couple of hours, asking me to get them this and that—then leave a 50 cent or dollar tip, like they're doing me a big favor! I *feel* like saying something smart to them, but I don't. I've learned to smile and say 'thank you,' acting as though the one dollar bill is a ten. And the next time they come in, I'm just as nice. You've got to treat customers (and your boss and co-workers) graciously if you want to do well in the long-run."

Think of your lunch break as the ideal time to get "non-business" things done. Use it for running personal errands, or go to the local Y to play a round of racketball or get in a swim. Similarly, your commuting time can be put to good use. If you drive to work, listen to upbeat, motivational or instructional tapes, or books on tape. If you take the bus, subway or train (or carpool with people who prefer to forgo early morning chit-chat), use the time to write letters to friends, or read. If you live within walking distance of the office, walk *briskly* (good exercise!) and use the time to mentally organize your day.

Even the most exciting job has its dull moments (some have more than their share). If you find yourself dreading getting out of bed and heading to work, rethink your "work attitude." With the right mindset, you can turn even the most boring aspects of your job into almost-enjoyable ones. Kate Cusick spent hours photo-copying "boards" (illustrations and texts of TV commercials) in her ad agency job. "Standing at the Xerox machine for 20 or 30 minutes was so tedious at first," she concedes. "Then I started *reading* the boards—each had 'cartoon' figures with captions—and they were very interesting. I was able to learn more about the ad industry—the way people put the ads together—just by read-ing the boards while I photocopied them."

EIGHT ON-THE-JOB MISTAKES THAT CAN GET YOU CANNED (OR DEMOTED)

Everybody makes mistakes—but the smart people learn from (and correct) them. Here are the most common on-the-job errors.

1. *Coming to work late.* It's 9 A.M. and your co-workers are already at their desks, hard at work. Everyone's in place—except you. Yes, you overslept, again (or, your car broke down for the third time this week, or your dog ate your bus ticket), and you sidle in at 9:10 or 9:15. *You* may not view this tardiness as a vice. After all, you were late to *class* plenty of times and the teacher always excused you because you were an A student and you always got your work done on time. But in Corporate America, tardiness is one of the top complaints bosses have about employ-

ees (we even know of *one* boss who patrols the hallways at 9 A.M. sharp to take a head count!).

2. *Doing a disappearing act.* Unless you have a job where you're expected to be away from your desk, running errands or acting as an "internal" messenger, try to stay at or near your desk for a good part of the workday. And, avoid running out to get a cup of coffee at the deli across the street, returning late from lunch, spending 10 minutes—instead of two—in the washroom, or hanging out at the water cooler. If you're away from your desk alot, your bosses (and colleagues) will think you're sloughing off.

3. *Coming on too strong.* You may be the "life of the party" when you're with friends, or known as the "class clown" at school, but tone down your act at the office. And, check your voice level—some people have a tendency to talk too loudly, which annoys both bosses and co-workers alike. It's likely you'll share a "cubicle" or workspace with others, so keep your voice down when talking with someone or making a phone call; otherwise, your colleagues won't be able to hear themselves think.

4. *Interrupting.* If you're prone to breaking in on other people's conversations to offer your own wise and witty thoughts, get out of the habit. Learn to think before you speak—especially if you're just about to break in on your *boss's* conversation. Avoid giving others the impression you're "mouthy" or must always be the center of attention. And practice *listening* rather than talking— you'll be surprised at how much you can learn from others.

5. *Gossiping.* There's always at least *one* office gossip, the person who dishes the juiciest dirt about colleagues, bosses, top management. While it's okay to keep an ear tuned to what's going on around the office, avoid the temptation to participate directly in spreading the bad word about someone (inevitably, it'll get back to them). Keep your nose clean—you want to be an employee others can trust with their confidences.

6. *Calling your girlfriend, boyfriend—any friend—on company time.* We recently heard about one young woman who was on

the phone so often making personal calls that her boss threatened to yank the cord out of the wall! (Her co-workers were tempted to wrap it around her neck.) It's fine to make a quick call to your mom to let her know you'll be late for dinner, or to a friend to arrange to meet after work. But keep personal calls to a minimum, and *never* make personal long-distance calls from the office. Not only will you cost the company money—a long-distance call *may* cost you your job; many corporations now have monitoring systems that record long-distance calls and the extension they're made from.

7. *Whining, cranking and moaning.* It's okay to occasionally commiserate with fellow employees about long hours, low pay, tough assignments, but keep complaints to a minimum. Above all, don't let your bosses hear you griping. If you seem dissatisfied with your job, your boss may ask you to "look elsewhere" for employment, or she simply may not ask you to "join the team" *next* summer.

8. *Imitating "Pig Pen."* Yes, we mean the character in the *Peanuts* cartoon strip, the little guy who's always surrounded by a cloud of dust. Keep your desk and work area tidy and clean. Avoid stacking piles of papers on your desk (arrange papers neatly in a "to do" box). Don't leave half-eaten donuts, sandwiches or salads on your desk, intending to finish them off later. And be sure to leave the office kitchen or coffee area neat and clean. Avoid stashing dirty mugs in the sink, hoping some kindly soul will wash them for you. If you take the last cup of coffee, rinse out the pot and make fresh coffee for the next person (your co-workers will thank you for this!).

ASKING FOR—AND GETTING—
A RAISE OR PROMOTION

If you're a summer employee, whether you get a raise or promotion during those first couple of months depends to a large degree on your company and your boss. Many businesses start summer workers out at minimum wage ($4.75 an hour), and raises simply aren't an option—though you *can* ask for more money if you return the following summer. If you work at a year-round job, however, and feel you've done outstanding work, you can approach your boss after six months and ask for a raise (or promotion, if you feel you're ready to handle more responsibility).

Most companies will tell you when they hire you how soon you'll be up for a "review." Some businesses evaluate employees every six months, others once a year. If your boss doesn't mention review or evaluation schedules when you hire on, ask her about the company's policy regarding reviews, raises, and promotions.

If your company does have a set review policy, you're in luck; when the six-month (or one-year) mark rolls around, make an appointment to speak with your boss—and be prepared to list *all* your on-the-job accomplishments. Don't be modest—at raise-time, you *want* to blow your own horn; the same applies when asking for a promotion. If you're feeling nervous, *rehearse* what you want to say before you actually sit down with the boss. For example, tell her how you've totally redone the filing system so other employees have easier access to records, or if you're a department store clerk, how you managed to rack up sales of $300 to $500 most days.

If your company doesn't have a set review policy, it'll be up to you to make the first move. The best time to do this is six months after you've joined the company, or right after you've completed a major project, or received numerous compliments on your work from customers or superiors. Be aware that *timing* is a key factor when it comes to getting a raise or promotion. Before sauntering into your boss's office and asking for a pay hike, consider how your request jibes with current events on the office front. Is the company starting to lay off workers? Did the business just post record profits—or losses? If layoffs and losses are on the rise, this is definitely *not* the right time to ask for a raise!

Also, consider your boss's mood. Has she just lost an important pitch for new business? Is *her* boss coming down hard on her for some reason? If so, she probably won't be anxious to sit down and talk about how *you* can improve your standard of living. On the other hand, did your boss just win kudos from management for her outstanding sales presentation? Was she chosen "employee of the month"? Then charge ahead—she's probably feeling more benevolent than usual.

After six or so months on the job, you'll probably be able to pick up on the times when your boss is most receptive to granting your wishes. One teen recalls how her boss was always "in a really grouchy mood on Mondays. We knew not to pitch any new ideas to him before Wednesday, when he'd started to warm up a little. And we always saved our really big requests for Friday afternoons when he was in a mellow pre-weekend mood. He was also an ardent baseball fan, so I learned as much as I could about the sport and after I'd been working for eight months, I walked into his office and said, 'Hey, did you see how the Sox trounced the Indians Monday night?' That led to a half hour conversation about baseball (I let him do most of the talking, since my baseball expertise was still in its infancy!). Then, when he was good and relaxed, I eased into the subject of both a raise and a promotion. It was almost like taking candy from a baby— I got both!"

This teen was lucky—and she understood her boss. Be careful you don't barge in on your employer and expect him to talk about money then and there. If he's unprepared, you'll make him feel put on the spot, and he'll probably nix your request. Instead, choose a moment when he's feeling relaxed; then ask if you can make an appointment to talk with him at a "convenient time." This will give both of you time to organize your thoughts.

When asking for a raise, arm yourself with the knowledge of what you can fairly expect to be earning. What do teens in your position at other related businesses pull down? Do you know what your office counterparts are making? Having a general sense of what the market will bear guarantees that you won't undersell yourself—or lose your credibility by asking for three times what you're worth. Once you've done your homework, *do* ask for a little more money than you expect to get. This will allow your boss some room to negotiate and enable you to "compromise" and accept a lower sum.

Ideally, your boss will come through with the raise you want— or promote you to a new position. But what if she denies your request? Or, your raise is so minuscule it'll barely pay for one new CD a month? Or, your "promotion" consists of added "paper-pushing" rather than *real* responsibility?

Keep your cool, no matter how disappointed or angry you feel. Either accept your boss's decision, then raise the subject of more money or a better job again in a few months, or *quietly* start looking for a new job. Don't threaten to quit—unless you already have a signed and sealed offer from another company. And, even if you do leave, don't storm off in a huff your last day. Be sure to give a two-week notice and explain rationally and nicely to your boss *why* you're accepting a job offer at another company. Also, ask your boss how you can make things easier for the person who takes your place (you might even volunteer to accept a few phone calls from your replacement once he starts work—if he needs you to explain where files are located, for example). Above all, try to be on good terms with your boss when you leave your job; you never know when you'll have to call on him for a reference—you might even end up working for or with him at another company years later.

Fortunately, such leave-taking is almost never necessary. If you're good at what you do, and have proven a good "fit" with the company, management will want to keep you around. After all, they've just spent six months of their time and money training you. Chances are, they won't want to see that investment walk out their door and through that of their biggest competitor.

WILL YOU HAVE TO FILE A TAX RETURN?

You must file a tax return (form 1040), regardless of whether you think you owe any money or expect a refund, if your earned income totals more than $3,400 in a calendar year (January 1 through December 31). The formula changes if you receive any *unearned* income, such as interest from a bank account or stock dividends. In that case, you'll need to file a return if *your earned and unearned income totals more than $550* (note: amounts change every year. For more info, contact your local IRS— Internal Revenue Service—office).

If filing a tax return gives you a case of insomnia, a quick review of IRS publication No. 17, *Your Federal Income Taxes* (available at local IRS offices), will lull you to sleep with an up-to-date explanation of the taxability of your income and the deductibility of business-related expenses.

Tip Tips

If part of your income is made up of tips, you'll need to report that amount when you file your income tax return. For specific how-tos, pick up IRS Publication No. 531, *Reporting Income From Tips.*

8

Managing It All

Keeping it all together—juggling work, school, and family and social commitments—can be tough. Many times it'll seem as if there simply aren't enough hours in the day—and you'll find yourself trying to cram *everything* in.

SCHEDULING YOUR TIME

Zakia Andrews, who ran her own business selling lingerie at "Tupperware-like" parties and worked a part-time job when she was in high school, admits that her hectic pace sometimes left her feeling stressed out. But she learned to set priorities and stick to a strict weekly schedule. "I kept a weekly planner where I listed *everything*—school, social and work-related activities. From 8 A.M. to 1 P.M., I went to school. From 1:30 to 4 P.M., I concentrated on homework, or just rested. From 4 to 8 P.M., I worked at The Gap. In my spare time, I scheduled trips to New York City (from my hometown, Philadelphia) to buy merchandise for my business; organized and held the parties; or got together with friends. By sticking to a schedule, knowing where I was supposed to be and when, I cut down on that stressed-out feeling. I wasn't constantly thinking, 'Oh, no! I forgot to do such and such!' "

Take Zakia's lead and buy a weekly or monthly planner. Get one with spaces large enough to list all your activities, projects and appointments for each day—that way, one calendar will keep you on track.

SET PRIORITIES

If you do begin to feel as though your job or business is "taking over your life," and your schoolwork's suffering, or your social life is nil, or you begin to feel rundown or get attacks of stress-related symptoms (frequent headaches, stomachaches, anxiety attacks), take stock of the situation. You may need to do some reorganizing—or cut back on your work hours. It's important that each area of your life balance the other; work, school, family and friends should all come together to form a well-rounded lifestyle.

"No one area, be it work or social life, or whatever, should dominate," says Lana Israel, 16, who runs a Miami-based publishing company, but gives equal time to schoolwork and activities. Lana's active in student government, having served as sophomore class president and vice president of the student council. She's also a member of her high school volleyball team, the soccer team, the debate society, and has played alto sax and flute in the school band.

"I make sure I have a social life, as well as a professional one," Lana says. "I think everyone should be well-rounded; as soon as one area starts to dominate your life, you can become overwhelmed. That's when it's time to step back, to set priorities and modify your lifestyle."

MAKING TIME FOR FAMILY AND FRIENDS

Paramedic Sal DiMeglio has one of the roughest schedules imaginable—attending college classes five days a week, studying, and working 30 or more hours a week treating victims of various emergencies. "It's hard," he says, "but you make time for the important things or people in your life. I have a girlfriend, and when I work a midnight shift, often instead of going home and crashing, I'll go see her."

Friendships are an important part of Sal's life as well. He says, "While I may not see my friends from high school every day—as I did in the past—I try to make the most of the few hours we have together every couple of weeks or so. I try to maintain those ties, and whenever we're together we have a great time."

Sal feels it's also important to maintain close family ties. "My dad's a chef and he doesn't get home until 11 P.M. six nights a week. Often, he's coming home just as I'm leaving to go to work. I try to call him at the restaurant a few times a week just to catch up. And when I come in after working the midnight shift, I wake him so we can talk. He never minds me waking him up."

KEEPING YOUR SOCIAL LIFE ALIVE AND WELL

Don't let friendships fall by the wayside because you're frantically trying to juggle heavy work and school schedules. Here are some tips for maintaining friendships (romantic or otherwise).

Make seeing friends a priority. Plan to get together with one (or more) good friends during the week or on the weekend.

Schedule meaningful activities you're 99 percent sure you'll enjoy. If going to "Roger's party" on Saturday night fills you with dread (or causes a case of the "yawns"), politely decline and plan to spend the evening doing something you *really* want to do, with someone you *really* want to be with.

When you're extremely swamped and can't get together with friends, keep in touch. Try these methods:

- Remember, the telephone provides fast access. Call your friend—especially if you think she feels you've been neglecting her.
- If you and a friend have access to personal computers, have your computer call his computer. Leave a message: "Want to see the new movie at the Bijou Saturday night? If so, leave a message on my P.C. by noon, Friday."
- Write notes or letters to close friends (even if they live three houses away!). We know of two high school seniors who are so busy with part-time clerking jobs, sports activities, schoolwork and church activities, they hand notes (or, more accurately, long letters) to each other when they pass in the halls at school. Says one, "It's our way of staying connected when our schedules are *crazy*."

STRESS-BUSTERS

Feeling overwhelmed? Or a little stressed? Here are 10 smart stress-busters that will also boost your energy level:

1. *Get in 30 minutes of aerobic exercise five times a week.* Sal says he relieves his job- and school-related stress by playing ice hockey "with some guys from high school as well as some local cops and firefighters. The physical activity really helps us get rid of our tension."

Studies show that vigorous physical activity causes the brain to release endorphins, "natural tranquilizers" that calm you and help restore emotional equilibrium. Any aerobic activity, such as brisk walking, jogging, playing tennis, hockey, or basketball, aerobic dance, swimming or jumping rope will cut your stress quotient quickly.

2. *Set aside private time.* When Linda Menzies worked full time as a graphic designer—and ran her part-time design business in her "off-hours"—she set aside one day a week to spend on herself, and forget about work. "I physically—and mentally—got away from the pressures of work," she says. You can "escape" too, by taking in a movie, going for a long walk, reading an absorbing book, or just soaking in a deliciously scented tub.

3. *Learn a relaxation technique.* Take a class in yoga or meditation. Or try this easy deep-breathing exercise: Find a quiet place and sit in a comfortable chair, with your feet on the floor, your arms at your sides. Breathe in deeply, filling your diaphragm, not just your lungs. As you breathe out, repeat the sound "ommmmmmm" or a meaningful word or phrase. Continue breathing in and out, slowly and deeply, for five to 20 minutes.

4. *Schedule "worry time."* Set aside 30 minutes every day to concentrate on everything that's bothering you (from the paper you have to write for history to the fight you had with your girlfriend to the way your boss criticized you yesterday because your work was late). When worries crop up during the day, promise yourself you'll handle them during your worry session. End

each session with a positive visualization, imagining yourself successfully overcoming your "challenges."

5. *Follow a smart, healthy diet.* Include daily choices from the four basic food groups: dairy; fruit/veggie; grain; protein. Make sure you eat *three* meals a day—and remember, breakfast should be your biggest meal; a nutritious breakfast including juice, cereal, and yogurt or milk will make you more alert and more productive during the A.M. hours.

6. *Limit caffeine and sugar intake.* Both can send you soaring, then plunging, as your blood sugar drops. If you *do* drink coffee, combine it with a complex carbohydrate food, such as whole-grain bread or a whole-grain muffin. The caffeine will make you mentally alert, while the carbos will calm you and keep you on an even keel.

7. *Take a multi-vitamin daily, if you feel you aren't eating enough fruits or veggies.*

8. *Laugh.* Researchers have found that laughter provides psychological relief from tension, anxiety, anger and emotional pain. To boost your laughter quotient, rent funny movies or tapes of your favorite stand-up comic. Read humorous stories or flip through joke books.

9. *Make sure you get enough shut-eye.* Most teens need a good eight hours (did you know your body actually "repairs" itself while you sleep?). If you find you're waking up in the middle of the night, or can't fall asleep in the first place, try these sleep-inducing tips:

- Go to bed and get up at the same time every day, even on weekends. If you stay up too late—or sleep in—you can disrupt your normal sleep cycle.
- About five hours before bedtime, get in a half hour of exercise (don't exercise right before going to bed—you'll end up feeling overly energized).
- A few hours before bedtime, relax in a comfortably warm tub.
- Avoid eating dinner after 7 P.M. Digestion revs up your

heart rate and can keep you awake. If you *do* crave a bedtime snack, treat yourself to a glass of warm milk or a whole-grain muffin or toast—all will help you feel drowsy.

· Avoid drinking caffeinated beverages (this includes colas) after 2 P.M. Caffeine can disrupt sleep patterns in certain people.

10. *If you're feeling very stressed out—or depressed—share your feelings with a close friend or a school counselor or a clergy-person.* Sometimes just talking about your problems will help you feel better about life; another, objective person can also help you gain some perspective on your problems.

9

Are *You* an Entrepreneur?

- You'd like to run your own business.
- You want to answer to yourself—not to a boss.
- You want to be independent.
- You prefer your work time to be flexible—and planned by you, not by someone else.

You've thought it over, and you're 90 percent sure you'd like to become self-employed—to join the thousands of other enterprising teens across the U.S. who run their own businesses. But you still have some questions: Are you cut out for entrepreneurship? Will you be able to handle the risks—and the opportunities—of going into business for yourself? Have you got the skills, the terrific ideas, the motivation to start and successfully run a business?

Take this quick quiz to discover your entrepreneurial potential:

SELF-ANALYSIS

1. Are you a leader?   Yes   No
2. Do you like to make your own decisions?   Yes   No
3. Do you enjoy competition?   Yes   No
4. Do you have willpower and self-discipline?   Yes   No
5. Do you plan ahead (instead of putting things off)?   Yes   No

6. Do you like people?   Yes   No

7. Do you understand that a lot of hard work will be involved in running your own business?   Yes   No

8. Will you be able to juggle your business responsibilities with school, family and social commitments?   Yes   No

9. Do you have a positive attitude, one that will help you handle the strain of running a business?   Yes   No

10. Are you prepared, if needed, to temporarily cut back on unnecessary expenses (money you shell out for movies, concerts, new clothes, dates)?   Yes   No

11. Do you feel your family will support your decision to start your own business?   Yes   No

12. Are you prepared to put some upfront money into a business—and risk losing it?   Yes   No

PERSONAL SKILLS AND EXPERIENCE

13. Do you know what basic skills you'll need to run a successful business?   Yes   No

14. Do you possess those skills?   Yes   No

15. If your business expands, and you need to hire people to work for you, will you be able to determine whether their skills meet your requirements?   Yes   No

16. Have you ever been in a managerial or supervisory role (managing a fast-food restaurant, organizing school activities)?   Yes   No

17. Have you ever worked at a business similar to the one you want to start?   Yes   No

18. Have you taken any business classes in school?   Yes   No

19. If you discover that you don't have the skills needed for your business, would you be willing to put your plans on hold until you've learned those skills?   Yes   No

Now, total up your points. For each "yes" answer, give yourself 10 points, for each "no," zero points. If you scored between 170 and 190 points, you possess an "entrepreneurial personality." If your points total 140 to 170, you have a pretty good chance of getting your business off the ground—but you'll need to work extra hard to keep it going. If your score is 140 or below, we suggest you give Corporate America a try first; once you've got some work experience, then consider starting your own business.

WHAT QUALITIES DO
SUCCESSFUL ENTREPRENEURS SHARE?

* They're typically leaders, rather than followers.
* They thrive on competition—and need to achieve.
* They're high-energy people, able to work long hours and juggle a multitude of responsibilities.
* They like to be in the spotlight, to be recognized for what they accomplish.
* They're risk-takers, choosing challenge over security.
* They're goal-oriented, setting goals and then doing everything possible to reach those goals (they believe in the philosophy, "Stick to it until you do it!").
* They're "practical dreamers," able to recognize profitable opportunities (where others see none), but also capable of implementing a practical plan to turn those opportunities—their dreams—into reality.
* They possess a high level of self-esteem and are confident they can do whatever they set their minds to.

10

Start with a Winning Idea

"It seemed like a good idea," says 11-year-old Monique Rollins of her decision to market her specially designed tee shirts. "I take art lessons, and I'd designed tee shirts for friends and relatives for their birthdays," she explains. When Monique's unique tees drew rave reviews from the recipients, she realized there was a potential "market" for her work.

At 10, she started buying space at various craft fairs and sold tees, sweatshirts, totebags, and baseball caps. Working freehand with "slick paint" (it's got a slightly rubbery texture), she tailors her designs to the public's tastes. "If I've bought space at our local ice rink (during a skating competition), I'll sell tees picturing ice skates or a girl skating on a lake." At craft fairs, Monique has found that items with music themes (a violin or music notes emblazoned on a tote), animal prints (racoons, cats), fish pictures and peacocks sell well. Monique also creates abstract designs and often presses rhinestones, faux pearls, and beads ("from my old jewelry and my mom's") into the paint.

What began as a hobby—designing tees for gifts—has turned into a profitable business for Monique, who sells her tees for $20 and her sweatshirts for $25.

Every business begins with a good idea. Notice we said "good," not "brilliant," though some ideas are touched by genius. (See the

Casey Golden and Lana Israel stories in this chapter for examples!) An idea that translates into a profitable business doesn't need to be new—often, you can take an old idea and make it "new" for *you*. Remember how Oren Jenkins came up with the notion of starting his own lawn service? Mowing grass is hardly a new concept—and certainly not a brilliant one—but Oren *saw a need and filled it*. He noticed that his elderly neighbors (and there were many) weren't able to tend to their lawns; he also realized that the commercial lawn services charged high rates. Oren figured he could undercut the competition by offering quality work at reduced rates—and within a month or two, his successful business was born.

PRACTICE CREATIVE THINKING

How can you come up with an idea for a business? One that works for you? Start by making a list of all your talents and interests—your experience, your knowledge, the things you enjoy *doing*, all come into play when you're searching for your ideal business. For instance, if you're in all the school plays, if you love entertaining people, and you enjoy little kids, you might decide to start a "birthday party business" by taking your clown act or magic show into the homes of neighborhood children (good acts can pull in $25 to $50). Love animals? Think about launching a pet-walking or pet-sitting service.

Take Oren's lead and look around your neighborhood or community and find a *need*—then fill it. Are the kids at your school constantly asking to borrow a pencil or paper because they haven't had time to stop by a stationery store to pick up necessary items? We know of one 13-year-old who started his own "school supply" business peddling pencils, pens, notebooks, paper, erasers and various other items to fellow students (with the school's blessing—possibly because the *teachers* were tired of having students ask to borrow things!). He bought his merchandise for wholesale prices through his dad's office supply store, then sold it at a 50 percent markup.

Are you the type of person who's constantly coming up with great ideas—only to forget them? Carry a pad and pencil in your pocket or tote. Whenever you have *any* idea—no matter how silly it may seem—jot it down for future reference. Keep a pad and pencil by your bed, too. Sometimes when we're really relaxed and ready to drift off, brilliant ideas hit (others of us get our best ideas in the A.M. when we're just waking up).

"MR. TEE"

"When I was ten, one of my grade school teachers gave our class an assignment: come up with a problem, then solve it," says 13-year-old Casey Golden of Evergreen, Colorado. "My biggest problem at the time was having to pick up my dad's broken golf tees when I caddied for him. My dad explained that the tees could dull or damage the lawnmower blades—or if they hit just right, pop a flat tire.

"I'd wondered for a long time why someone couldn't invent a golf tee that just 'disappeared' into the ground when the sprinklers went on, or it rained."

Casey set about doing just that. Using a concoction of flour, water, peat moss, fertilizer, grass seed and applesauce, he created a "biodegradable golf tee" that was strong enough to hold a golf ball, but soft enough to dissolve and be absorbed into the soil. He then entered the tee in Invent America, a nationwide contest for kids, K-8, and won $1,000. But that was only the beginning of his success story. Casey's dad, John, recognized the marketing potential of his son's invention—and quit his job as an insurance sales rep to form a company, Biodynamics, that makes and sells the BIO-T. "We had to test a lot of variations of the original formula," says Casey, noting that golf course owners weren't crazy about the grass seed component since they didn't want "strange" grass sprouting on their pristine greens!

Casey and his father hired a patent attorney and worked with a group of chemists to formulate the final "recipe." Casey says, "We applied for a patent in December of 1990 and it was issued in '91."

Today, when he's not busy with junior high classes or after-school activities such as basketball and golf, Casey speaks to groups of "young inventors" around the country. He's even traveled to Japan to speak to a group of parents, teachers and kids. As a stockholder in Biodynamics, Casey occasionally goes on "sales calls" with his dad (the company sells the BIO-T to golf courses, pro shops, sporting goods stores and the K-Mart chain). Currently, Casey and his father are working with a major chemical company to create other biodegradable products based on the BIO-T formulation.

What's the best advice Casey can offer other young inventors? "Try your best, and if your invention doesn't work right away don't get discouraged. Make another variation of it—or a dozen variations. It took Thomas Edison almost 10,000 tries before he got the light bulb to shine for more than a minute!"

Have *you* invented something? Protect your invention by applying for a patent. Patents are available by number for $1.50 from the Patent and Trademark Office, Washington, D.C. 20231.

Books Are Her Business

Sixteen-year-old Lana Israel, of North Miami Beach, Florida, turned an eighth-grade science project into an amazingly successful business venture.

"When I was 13, my father gave me a book called Use Both Sides of Your Brain by Tony Buzan." Buzan had developed an innovative learning technique called Mind Mapping that intrigued Lana. "It sounded like a great method, but I wondered if it would really work, and if it could be applied to education," says Lana, who decided to devote her science project to Mind Mapping principles. The project was a great success and was presented at local and state science fairs. One of Lana's former teachers saw the project and was so impressed she asked if the teen would be interested in making a presentation at a seminar for educators in Sydney, Australia. Lana and her teacher faxed the project materials to the conference officials, and two summers ago, Lana became the first teen to make a presentation at the Eighth World Conference for Gifted and Talented Children.

BRIGHT IDEAS!

Products to Make and Sell:

- Greeting cards, stationery, hand-painted or stenciled gift-wrap
- Hand-painted or silk-screened tees, sweatshirts, sneakers, totes, baseball caps, baby clothes, socks
- A neighborhood or community cookbook, with recipes from men, women and children
- A community "restaurant" cookbook, with the chefs' favorite recipes
- Cookies, pies, cakes, candies
- Iced tea, iced coffee, lemonade, fruit "slushes" (sell during the summer). Hot chocolate, hot cider, "flavored" coffees (sell during the winter).
- Costume jewelry made from metals, rhinestones, fake pearls, beads, buttons, and unusual materials such as laquered paper

---

"My teacher said many of the presenters would have photocopied materials to distribute to the educators attending the conference, so I put my materials together in book form—and called it Brain Power for Kids: How to Become an Instant Genius. The book explains how we learn—and what's wrong with our current learning methods—then goes on to tell how we can use Mind Mapping to increase our learning, improve study habits, get better grades. I received a lot of press coverage in Sydney, and as a result, an Australian company published my book for distribution throughout that country and New Zealand."

Like many about-to-be entrepreneurs, Lana didn't realize she was sitting atop a gold mine. "I'd wanted to start my own business for a long time (I'd taken several courses focusing on entrepreneurship)," she says. "Then my dad bought me a copy of The Busine$$ Kit (published by Busine$$ Kids/America's Future)—and that got me excited. The kit gave how-tos for starting a business and the final part concentrated on coming up with an idea for a business. At that point, I got a little discouraged, since none of the ideas struck me as something I wanted to devote a lot of time to."

But soon after she put The Busine$$ Kit aside, Lana realized she "didn't have to come up with an idea. I already had a potential business. In the States, I'd been giving my book away. I suddenly realized I could sell the book—there was a market for it. That's when I officially started my company, Brain Power for Kids, Inc."

Lana borrowed $7,000 from her dad (she's since paid him back in full) and self-published her book (in conjunction with Buzan). In addition to explaining the Mind Mapping technique, the book includes activities to help the reader improve his learning skills.

"I did everything myself—the writing, illustrations, layouts, proofreading. Then I took the manuscript to a local printer and had 3,000 copies run off," Lana explains.

Lana describes herself as "a very positive person. I didn't worry too much about the boxes and boxes of books sitting in my house, going nowhere for a couple of months. I knew there was a market for them because I'd gotten a large influx of letters about the book even before I self-published." Lana credits "the media" with doing most of her advertising—and generating advance sales. She's appeared on local and national TV shows and has been interviewed by numerous newspapers. As part of her business, she makes frequent presentations to schools, summer camps, and private learning centers. "I've gotten quite a few bulk orders from schools," she notes.

BRIGHT IDEAS!

Products to Buy in Bulk and Sell at a Profit
* Pens, pencils, bookcovers, notebooks, tape, staples, glue, erasers (sell to kids at school—you'll save them a trip to the stationery store)
* Baby clothes
* Lingerie (see Zakia Andrews' story, page 99)
* Book bags, totes, duffel bags
* Stickers (little kids will buy lots!)
* Jewelry
* Hats, mittens, gloves

Services You Can Sell
* Pet-walking or pet-sitting
* Personal shopper (running errands, buying groceries for elderly neighbors, busy moms, dual-career couples)
* Catering (making and delivering meals to working couples)
* Dog grooming
* Mother's helper (taking care of kids, doing light housework and some cooking)
* Babysitting
* Entertaining—magic shows, clown acts—at parties
* Lawn service
* Plant-sitting (caring for neighbors' plants while they're away)
* Snow shoveling, leaf raking
* House-sitting
* Tutoring
* Housecleaning
* Typing or word-processing service
* Music instruction
* Computer skills (see Morris Beyda's story, page 94)
* Bicycle repair
* Car washing
* Messenger service
* Chauffeur service (if you have your own car)
* Computer graphics (designing menus for local restaurants, stationery, business cards, fliers and brochures for community businesses and events)

To date, Lana has sold more than 10,000 copies of Brain Power for Kids in the States (she receives royalties from an Australian publishing company). "My business gives me the best of many worlds," she says. "I'm involved in things I really enjoy—English and writing, science, and public speaking."

Want to order your own copy of Lana's book? Send $7 (price includes shipping and handling) to Brain Power for Kids, P.O. Box 630503, Miami, FL 33163, or call 1-305-931-7095.

11

Keep It Legal: Laws that May Affect Your Business

FILING FOR A SOCIAL SECURITY NUMBER

Before you can go to work—whether you're employed by someone else or running your own business—you'll need to apply for a Social Security number. But first check with your parents; they may already have obtained a number for you in order to declare you as a tax deduction. If they haven't, simply call or stop by your local Social Security Administration office and ask for Form SS-5: Application for a Social Security Card. (It usually takes between two and four weeks to receive an S.S. number.)

SALES TAX

Depending on the laws of your state, and city or town, you may be required to charge sales tax on any merchandise you sell directly to customers (if you sell to stores, *they'll* collect sales tax). Laws regarding the taxability of merchandise vary from state to state, but many states do not require sales tax on food or beverage items. To find out how to apply for a *state sales tax permit,* call the Department of Taxation (you'll find it listed in the "blue pages" of your telephone book, under "State Government"). Check with your city or town clerk to find out whether you'll need to file for a *city sales tax permit.*

EMPLOYER I.D. NUMBER
If you hire employees for your business, you'll need to apply for an Employer Identification Number. Check with the Internal Revenue Service for specific guidelines. (Note: if you "sub-contract" work—pay someone on a project-by-project basis—that person isn't considered an "employee" and you needn't file for an employer number. For more on sub-contracting, see page TK).

UNEMPLOYMENT TAX NUMBER
If you hire employees, you'll also need to apply for a state unemployment compensation tax number. Call the local office of your State Unemployment Commission for info.

ZONING RESTRICTIONS
Most cities have zoning requirements for small businesses. Some will allow you to operate a business from your home, while others strictly forbid it. Some towns even have special regulations regarding the size of signs (for advertising purposes) and where they can be posted. To find out about zoning ordinances in your area, contact your local Chamber of Commerce, the U.S. Small Business Administration, or your town's department of planning and zoning.

REGISTERING YOUR COMPANY NAME
You'll want to register the name of your business with the county courthouse; by doing this, you make sure no one else in the county is operating a business under the same name. See your county clerk for details.

TAXES
As a self-employed teen, you'll have to file a tax return if you earn more than $3,400 during a calendar year (January 1 through December 31). You'll also be required to pay a self-employment tax to the government if you earn $400 or more during the calendar year (self-employment tax is equivalent to the social

security tax withheld from employee paychecks). For more info, stop by your IRS office and pick up these publications: No. 334, *Tax Guide for Small Businesses;* No. 533, *Self-Employment Tax;* and, if you go into direct sales, No. 911, *Tax Information for Direct Sellers.*

12

Smart Move: The Business Plan

Now that you've come up with a great idea for your business and know the legal requirements for running your own company, you're ready to turn your dream into reality. That means "putting it on paper," or, formulating a "Business Plan."

Many small businesses fail because the entrepreneurs didn't plan carefully before they opened their businesses. A sound business plan will give you a greater chance for success. Some teen-operated businesses do grow without benefit of a formal plan—in part because of luck, in part because of the casual nature of the business. For example, see Morris Beyda's story at the end of this chapter. He explains how his computer instruction venture thrived without a formal plan, and how he's *now* putting together a business plan that will give his company more direction, a clearer structure.

A business plan should describe in detail *what* you want to do and *how* you're going to do it. It should define your business, identify your goals, clarify your financial needs, target your "market" (the customers you want to reach), and define marketing strategies. By putting together a well-thought-out plan, you can spot potential problems *before* they develop and figure out ways to avoid them. Finally, if you do need to borrow money for your venture (a *few* banks will give loans to teens *if* a parent or guardian co-signs the loan application), a professional-looking plan will help convince lenders that your business has potential for success.

Here are the four areas a comprehensive business plan should include, according to the U.S. Small Business Administration (SBA):

1. *A Description of the Business:*

   - What type of business are you planning? What product or service will you sell?
   - What type of business opportunity is it? Seasonal? Year-round? Part-time?
   - Why do you think the business will be successful?
   - What are the growth opportunities?

2. *Marketing Plan:*

   - Who are your potential customers?
   - How will you attract them?
   - Who are your competitors? How are *their* businesses doing?
   - How will you promote sales? Through radio or newspaper ads? Fliers? Posters? Word-of-mouth recommendations?
   - If you sell products, where will you get your merchandise? Will you make it yourself? Buy from wholesalers?
   - Where will your business be located?
   - What factors should influence your choice of location?

3. *Organization Plan:*

   - Who will manage your business? You? Someone you hire? A parent?
   - Is your manager qualified? (If you plan to manage the business—which is likely when you first start out—list any previous experience that applies to the type of business you're launching.)

- If you plan to hire employees, how many will you need? To do what? (Most likely, you'll do all your own work, or sub-contract work on a project-by-project basis, though some teens do hire full- and part-time employees. See David Eilers' story, page 114.)
- If you do hire employees, what are your plans for hiring, salaries, benefits, training, supervision? These questions— except benefits—also apply to people whose work you sub-contract.
- How will you manage your finances and record-keeping requirements? (Most likely, you'll have to handle both yourself, unless you hire someone to do them for you; see Chapter 17 for accounting how-tos.)
- What consultants and specialists will you need? For what? (Casey Golden hired a group of chemists to help him formulate his final BIO-T "recipe," and a patent attorney to help in the patenting process. It's possible to get free advice from local businesspeople in related fields, as well as from the SBA.)
- What licenses and permits do you need? What federal, state or city regulations will affect your business?

4. *The Financial Plan:*

- What is your estimated income for the first year? Figure monthly for the first year; quarterly for the second and third years.)
- What will it cost to open and sustain your business for the first 18 months?
- What do you expect your cash flow to be during the first year? What will your quarterly cash flow be during the second and third years?
- When do you expect to "break even," and start showing a profit?

- How many sales will you need to make to turn a profit during the first year? The first three years? (If your business is "casual"—making and selling tee shirts, or operating a lawn service, for example—you'll have little or no "overhead" [paying employees, renting space], so you should see a profit within the first month or so.)
- What is the capital value of your equipment? (Your word processor, computer, typewriter, power mower, art equipment)
- What are your potential funding sources? Your own bank account? Your parents? Relatives? A bank?
- If you *do* plan to try for a loan, will one of your parents co-sign for you? Do they have collateral (assets) the bank will accept?

We've outlined what goes into a fairly sophisticated business plan—the kind adults put together when they start small companies. You can play around with it, eliminating what doesn't apply to your venture. For example, you may not hire employees or sub-contract work, or, you might want to give your business only six months or a year to break even, rather than hanging in for a year and a half to see if you're going to make a go of it.

Here's a simplified plan we've put together for a girl—we'll call her "Terry"—who wants to start a tee-shirt business. Terry isn't seeking a loan from anyone, so an informal plan is all she needs to clarify her goals for *herself*.

TERRY'S TERRIFIC TEES

1. *Description of the Business:* I plan to decorate tee shirts, using paints and beads. My business will be called "Terry's Terrific Tees." I will operate it year-round, though I expect my best sales in July and August when the demand for tees is highest.

2. *Marketing:* I'll sell my tees at craft fairs, cooperative art

shows, community festivals and at my school. I also plan to sell some tees to the Bon Ton Shop in Girard, Ohio. My customers will be grade-school children, teens and adults.

a. My direct competition will come from other designers who sell their tees at craft fairs and art shows; I'm familiar with their merchandise and feel I can produce tees of equal or better quality.

I also will compete on a limited basis with ABC-Tee in Girard. ABC does a lot of business and is frequently sold out of fast-moving merchandise. I feel I can attract customers away from ABC by 1) selling my tees for $5 less; 2) by offering tees made of 100 percent high-quality cotton, instead of a polyester-cotton blend; and 3) by custom-designing special-order tees.

b. I will advertise my tee shirts in the local *Pennysaver;* post colorful signs at my school, the grocery store, and my church; and distribute fliers (which I will produce on my mother's computer) to houses within a 100-block radius of my home.

c. I plan to operate the business out of my house, using a corner of the basement for my work. My neighborhood is zoned for small, home-operated businesses.

3. *Organization:*

a. I will be the sole owner. I will manage the business and design all the tees.

I have an extensive art and graphic design background, having taken design, painting and silk-screening courses for the past five years. In addition, I've designed tees for the Bon Ton for the past two years.

b. I will handle all record-keeping duties, using a simple accounting system (my mother is a bookkeeper and has agreed to teach me the basics).

c. I plan to obtain state and city sales tax permits, which will give me access to tee-shirt wholesalers.

4. *Financial Plan:*

    a. I will use $100 from my savings account to cover start-up costs: 40 tees, paints, beads, rhinestones, rent for space at art and craft fairs.

    b. I plan to buy tee shirts at wholesale prices: $10 for 5 plain tees. I will sell my decorated tees for $20 apiece at art shows, fairs, at my school, and for $15 to Bon Ton.

    c. I expect sales to total $2,400 for the first year. (Based on what my competitors bring in at craft shows, I estimate I'll make approximately $800 from January through May, and between $1,600 and $1,700 from May through December.)

MORE BUSINESS PLAN HOW-TOS

The Small Business Administration offers publications that explain, in detail, how to draft a business plan. To order the following, call 202-205-6665, between 10 A.M. and 3 P.M., EST, Monday through Friday, or stop by your local SBA office:

The Business Plan For Home-based Business, MP15, $1.

Developing a Strategic Business Plan, MP21, $1.

COMPUTING BIG BUCKS

Morris Beyda, 17, is one of those people who "grew" a business before he developed an in-depth business plan. And Morris didn't need to look for a market—his target audience found him.

"I started my company, Computers Simplified, when I was 13," says the Dix Hills, New York, computer wizard. "I'd always been interested in computers, and many of my friends—and their parents—came to me for help in solving problems they were having with their computers. I taught them how to operate their equipment, how to set up various programs and advised them about what type of machine and software they should buy."

So many people were calling on Morris for his expertise, he decided to start charging for his services. "I had some business cards printed up, then charged $5 an hour for doing consulting work. I got the majority of my customers through word-of-mouth recommendations."

Today, the high school senior has a client base of 30 people and charges $30 an hour for most services, $20 for "phone consultations," and $40 for emergency services ("I carry a beeper and if a client has an emergency, he or she can get to me quickly"). In his first three years of business, Morris brought in $15,000.

Morris' customers are loyal, staying with him for a year or longer. "My first customer still calls me with emergencies—like problems with 'lost' files, or programs that aren't working right. I have customers who started calling me when they were in high school; now they're away at college and they call from campus with questions." Many of Morris' clients are adults. "At first, some are surprised when they see how young I am," he says, "but I've found that my age is actually an asset. I don't seem to intimidate them the way another adult might." Morris has also developed good people skills through his business dealings. "Some adults are almost afraid of computers," he says, "and I've learned to be very patient with them, to talk them through a program two or three times until they're comfortable with it. I try to personalize each lesson, taking the client's needs into account."

Morris kept cash flow records on his own computer from the day he began operating his business—but it's only now that he's formulating an actual business plan. "Up to now, my clients have been all over the map—kids, adults. By putting together a plan, I'm redefining my market, narrowing my focus, to the people I think I should be reaching. Increasingly, I'm working with college-bound high school seniors who want to purchase a computer to take with them. I'm planning to do some advertising at my school, and when I find out who my new customers are, I'll try to tailor a computer system to fit each of their needs. I've set up outlines of various computer systems they might be interested in, as well as deals they can get on computers and software through the university they plan to attend, or through local or mail order dealerships. Basically, it's a continuing analysis of what my clients want—and what I can provide.

"A business plan makes it easier for me to see what's happening overall. I now know exactly who I'm trying to reach and I can concentrate on that market."

WHERE KIDS CAN GET HELP!

Kids of all ages can join Busines$ Kids/America's Future for $9.95 a year. The Florida-based club teaches kids and teens about all facets of entrepreneurship, publishes a newsletter, holds workshops, and operates a toll-free hotline for members who need business advice.

The organization also offers a unique product called The Busines$ Kit, which consists of books that explain how to start and manage a business, plus a motivational audiocassette, stationery, business cards, and an appointment book. To order The Busines$ Kit, send $49.95, plus $8.50 shipping and handling, to: Busines$ Kids, 301 Almeria Ave., Suite 330, Coral Gables, FL 33134. (Checks and money orders are accepted.) Or call 1-800-852-4544 to order by phone (major credit cards are accepted).

13

Money Matters

"Start out small," advises Linda Menzies, "putting as little money as possible into your business at first." Avoid getting carried away—like the young man who decided to start a lawn service business and spent his $2,000 savings on a fancy riding mower and top-of-the-line hedge clippers. Since he made only $100 a week for the first year, it was several months before he saw any profits!

Another teen started her lawn service operation on a shoestring budget, using her *clients'* mowers and rakes (she did invest $100 in a pair of good-quality hedge clippers). She, too, brought in approximately $100 a week—and was able to quickly absorb the cost of the clippers, then spend some of her profits on a $250 power mower. At the end of six months, she *still* made $2,050!

KEEP START-UP COSTS DOWN

Try to get by with as little equipment and materials as possible in the beginning. If you plan to make and sell costume jewelry, for example, avoid buying beads, rhinestones, and other items at retail prices. Instead, buy them through a wholesaler, or better yet, make your first pieces using beads from your mom's old jewelry, from pieces you pick up for pennies at garage sales, and from ordinary items such as buttons.

Whenever you can, *borrow!* Need to produce 100 fliers? In-

stead of investing in a computer, borrow your parents' PC (if they have one) or get permission to use one of your school's machines.

Need office equipment or other tools? Buy used items in good working condition, For example, most typewriter repair shops offer bargains on rebuilt machines. Also check the classifieds for good deals on file cabinets, word processors, computers, power mowers.

TYPICAL START-UP COSTS INCLUDE:

- Beginning inventory (merchandise you plan to sell, or materials needed to make the merchandise)
- Equipment you need
- Space rental (unless you operate your business from home)
- Telephone hookup (unless you use your home phone)
- Promotion costs (for fliers, signs, ads on local radio, in newspapers)
- Fees for licenses or permits

PROJECT YOUR PROFITS

After you've formalized your business plan, the next step is putting together a "Sales Projection Chart," which will give you a fairly good idea of how much money you must put into your business each month, and how much you'll make in sales (you'll have to do a little guesswork here).

Before preparing her sales projection chart, Terry talked with several tee-shirt designers who regularly sell at craft fairs in the area; she based her projected sales on sales *those* people have reported during the past few years. Terry realizes that any number of variables could affect her sales for a given month. Because of rain, a major craft show might be cancelled (or postponed until the following month), or turnout for a fair may be low. On the other hand, a craft show might draw double the number of people expected, and Terry's sales could exceed her projection for a particular month.

Currently, Terry is paying $10 for five plain tees, but she expects the price to go up to $15 in the near future. She's wisely started reworking her sales projection chart on page 100 to reflect the price increase and its effect on her profits.

SIMPLE PLEASURES = NICE PROFITS
Eighteen-year-old Zakia Andrews came up with the idea of starting her own lingerie-sales business, Simple Pleasures, during a two-week "young entrepreneurs" seminar sponsored by Wharton, the prestigious business school at the University of Pennsylvania.

"We learned all about becoming an entrepreneur—from coming up with an idea to writing a business plan to managing the business," says Zakia. Each student received $50 to spend in New York City's wholesale district. "You could buy whatever you wanted," she explains, "then sell the merchandise at a flea market or art festival. The idea was to make a profit, which we'd then put back into our business."

SALES PROJECTION CHART

EXPENSES	June	July	August	September	October	November
Tees	20.00	40.00	40.00	20.00	20.00	20.00
Paints/beads	5.00	10.00	10.00	5.00	5.00	5.00
Promotion (fliers, *Pennysaver* ads)	2.00	2.00	2.00	2.00	2.00	2.00
Space rental at fairs	20.00	40.00	40.00	20.00	20.00	20.00
Total expenses per month	47.00	92.00	92.00	47.00	47.00	47.00
INCOME						
Tee-shirt sales	200.00	400.00	400.00	200.00	200.00	200.00
PROFITS PER MONTH (What you make after you deduct expenses)	153.00	308.00	308.00	153.00	153.00	153.00
CUMULATIVE PROFIT (Each month's profit added to the previous month's)	153.00	461.00	769.00	922.00	1075.00	1228.00

Zakia decided she wanted to sell lingerie at parties, informal affairs held in the homes of friends and relatives. But she needed more capital, so she presented her business plan, developed during the seminar, to Wharton's venture capital board. "They gave me $500 start-up money."

VENTURE CAPITAL

Need cash for your company? As we've already mentioned, a few banks will lend a small amount of money to teens *if* a parent co-signs the loan application, or the teen has considerable assets—stocks or bonds, for example.

A more likely source of capital will be parents or relatives who are willing to invest in your business. Show them a detailed business plan—they'll be more inclined to hand over their money! Lana Israel prepared a business plan for her publishing company *before* asking her dad to provide the start-up cash.

You might also raise capital by selling some of your belongings—things you don't need or use anymore. If you've outgrown your "kiddie computer"—and need a Mac for your business—sell your old machine (run an ad in the local paper, or post signs at local groceries and schools). Consider holding a "tag sale" in your front yard and unload that Nintendo set you haven't used in four years, your five-speed bike (especially if you get around by car these days!), books, dolls, outgrown clothing (especially coats)—anything you think your neighbors might buy. Ask your parents to contribute old appliances, clothes, books, etc., to the sale.

Once a month, the high school senior traveled by train from her hometown, Philadelphia, to New York City to buy wholesale merchandise. "My mom came with me to help carry all the bags," says Zakia, noting she made a conservative purchase for her first party—"just 30 pieces of lingerie."

"At the party, I showed my guests pictures of various items from the wholesalers' catalogues, and I got a pretty good idea of what I should buy for the next party." Since Zakia's guests ranged from teens to elderly women, she "tried to include items for each age group. I was also able to provide lingerie for large-sized women." Big sellers included underwear sets, camisoles, teddies, robes, slips, nightgowns and sports bras. Buying more and more merchandise for each party, Zakia pulled in approximately $400 a month and made $6,000 in one year.

Most of her customers came through word-of-mouth recommendations, but she also distributed fliers—designed on her computer—to friends and neighbors. "I drew a rose on pink paper, included the name of the business, the place and time of the party, and mentioned that door prizes would be handed out and refreshments served." She also generated some business through media exposure. "I've been featured in Essence Magazine, Black Enterprise and USA Today," says Zakia. "I've also appeared on local TV talk shows and was interviewed for an article that appeared in the Philadelphia Daily News."

Now a freshman majoring in radio, TV and film production at Philly's Temple University, Zakia's put her business temporarily on hold while she gets accustomed to her rigorous college schedule. Most likely she'll do just fine in college—or anything she sets her mind to. "I've had to learn to not be intimidated," she says. "The wholesalers in New York can be tough. At first, I didn't realize you had to bargain with them in order to make them come down in price. One of the people who regularly buys from the wholesalers taught me how to bargain—and I learned quickly that the sticker prices aren't what the wholesaler expects you to pay. I also learned that I had the upper hand. There are plenty of wholesalers and you can always go somewhere else for your merchandise. You just have to let them know you know it!"

SAVVY SEMINAR FOR SMART STUDENTS

In addition to taking part in Wharton's entrepreneurial seminar, Zakia also participated in an intensive four-day "High School Conference on Entrepreneurship," sponsored by EntreCon, an organization run by students affiliated with The Wharton School.

A unique program that brings together outstanding high school juniors and seniors from around the country, the conference focuses on the basics of business, specifics of the entrepreneurial process, and various methods and strategies for starting and running a business. Wharton professors and prominent entrepreneurs share their business expertise, experience and ideas with the conference participants.

For more info, write to: EntreCon 1992, Wharton Undergraduate Division, Suite 1100, Steinberg Hall-Dietrich Hall, Philadelphia, PA 19104-6375.

14

Tending to Business

Once you've launched your business, your next job is minding the day-to-day operations—everything from managing to organizing to hiring (you'll also need to keep accurate records, but we'll give you accounting how-tos in Chapter 17).

Being your own boss requires special skills and work habits. Are you ready? Take this quick quiz to see!

Circle the answer that best describes you, or how you usually react in certain situations:

1. When it comes to being a self-starter:

a. there's no job I can't plan by myself and see through as well.

b. I'm pretty uncomfortable unless I have someone to give me a clear idea of the task before I begin.

c. I can get started okay, but then I like to have someone fill in the bits and pieces I've forgotten.

2. When I start a project, even if it's a simple one, like putting hundreds of snapshots I've taken over the years into organized photo albums:

a. I figure I'll finish it someday.

b. I decide to complete it by next Christmas, when we have lots of company and my folks need the extra bed that the pictures are piled on.

c. I make a schedule and stick to it—nothing ever takes more than a few weeks.

3. I have a reasonable amount of confidence:

a. when I'm in a familiar situation and doing tasks I've done before.

b. when I'm in a completely new situation. In fact, I see it as a challenge and enjoy the excitement.

c. rarely; I approach challenging situations with a great deal of anxiety.

4. If I'm in a competitive situation, I:

a. think only of winning. I'll do anything within reason, and my code of ethics, to come out on top.

b. would like to win, but I'm much more interested in the competition as a learning experience.

c. don't mind winning, but sometimes I care more about other things.

5. If there's a crisis at school (for example, I was supposed to line up a commencement speaker and the person I got cancelled, so I have only two days to find a replacement), I find that:

a. I have plenty of energy, accomplish what I have to— and always get through the crisis in good shape.

b. I manage to stay on my feet, but just barely.

c. I usually have to turn to my parents, teachers, or friends to help me out.

6. When it comes to "meeting and greeting," I am:

a. shy enough to try to get someone else to handle my social responsibilities.

b. reasonably capable. I get knots in my stomach when, for example, I have to be the host of a party or make a speech.

c. definitely a "people person." I love to meet and greet.

7. When someone has to take charge of a project at school (heading up a committee, for example), I:

a. hope it will be my best friend because she'll give me something interesting to do.

b. desperately want the job myself—I know just how I'll manage it, so I volunteer to act as committee head.

c. would like to be in charge, but don't know how to speak up.

8. When things don't go my way:

a. I write it off to experience and learn from the failure—I'm confident that next time I'll do better.

b. I get really discouraged and kind of depressed for days.

c. I'm quite disappointed and try to explain it away; I might even blame someone else.

9. When I'm presented with the opportunity to learn something new (like operating my school's computer), I:

a. grab the opportunity, no matter what adjustments I have to make in my schedule. You never know when a new skill will come in handy.

b. try to make the time—if I can fit it into my social schedule.

c. usually pass, unless my parents or my teacher are very anxious to have me do it.

10. Ever since I was a little kid, people have described me as:

a. flexible, perhaps even a little wishy-washy.

b. rigid and unbending, even stubborn.

c. sure of myself, though always willing to listen to an expert opinion.

SCORING: Find the point value for each answer, then add up your points.

      1) a = 3,   b = 1,   c = 2
      2) a = 1,   b = 2,   c = 3
      3) a = 2,   b = 3,   c = 1
      4) a = 3,   b = 2,   c = 1
      5) a = 3,   b = 2,   c = 1
      6) a = 1,   b = 2,   c = 3
      7) a = 1,   b = 3,   c = 2
      8) a = 3,   b = 1,   c = 2
      9) a = 3,   b = 2,   c = 1
     10) a = 2,   b = 1,   c = 3

HOW YOU RATE: ARE YOU READY TO BE YOUR OWN BOSS?

A Captain of Industry (30 to 25 points): You definitely have "boss" skills. You should be able to motivate yourself, set and stick to schedules, and promote your business, since you have an abundance of confidence and enthusiasm and enjoy dealing with people.

On the Brink (24 to 18 points): You have a strong desire to become an entrepreneur (and to control your life and work), but you need to increase your self-esteem and motivation. Start your business gradually, and be sure to get advice from people-in-the-know (such as the experts at SCORE—we'll tell you about this helpful group on page 109).

Needs Work (17 to 10 points): You've got a good idea for a business, but you need to work on your confidence quotient. Reread Chapter 3 and practice the esteem-boosting techniques. You might also profit from a class in public speaking, as well as a course in goal-setting and risk-taking (some high schools and many community colleges offer these types of classes).

GETTING HELP

As a boss—even if you're "bossing" only yourself—you'll need lots of self-confidence, especially when it comes to dealing with other people—customers, suppliers, and should you need them, employees. If you scored a "2" or "1" on questions 3, 9 and 11, concentrate on upping your confidence level by taking a public speaking course at your school, a local community college, or the "Y." The more you're "on stage" presenting your ideas, the more comfortable you'll feel when dealing with the public and selling your product or service.

You can also counter your "shy side" with this simple technique psychologists often recommend to clients: Each week, make a point of meeting someone, of walking up and introducing yourself, then starting a conversation. Try this in class, school hallways, or at parties. After a couple of months, you'll find you're pretty adept at "meeting and greeting," and you may end up with new friends—or even customers for your business.

Do you have trouble talking with adults? Most likely, some of your customers and many of your suppliers will be in the "over-21" group. "Practice" on your parents' friends, striking up a conversation about something *they're* interested in, or asking for their advice about a project you're working on. They'll appreciate your sudden attentiveness (and they may send customers your way).

The more you know about business in general, the more confident you'll feel about running your own company. Become a well-informed businessperson by taking courses in budgeting, accounting, marketing, promotion and sales skills (check the course lists at local community colleges, as well as university-sponsored county cooperative extension services programs). Call the business school at your nearest university to see if it offers special seminars (such as Wharton's EntreCon Conference). Get into the habit of checking the "community events" section in your local newspaper; many list lectures and one-day seminars focusing on business-related topics. Read the "business" magazines: *Working Woman, Business Week, Success,* for example. Talk with local businesspeople to find out how they organize and manage *their* businesses, how they attract new customers, how they solve business problems. You'll find that many local business owners are happy to share their expertise with enthusiastic young entrepreneurs.

Stop by the nearest office of the U.S. Small Business Administration. The SBA offers many valuable services and programs for entrepreneurs, including training and educational programs, advisory services, publications, financial programs and specialized programs for women business owners and minority entrepreneurs. To locate your area SBA office, look in the telephone directory under U.S. Government, or call the Answer Desk at 1-800-U ASK SBA.

NEED EXPERT KNOW-HOW?

You can get *free* advice about starting and running a business from the experts at SCORE, the Service Corps of Retired Executives, a volunteer program of the SBA. Call your nearest SBA office and tell them what type of business you have (or plan to start), and they'll match you up with a volunteer who can help you identify basic management problems, determine the causes, and teach you how to become a *better* manager. SCORE counseling can also help you decide when, where, and how to expand your business. In addition, the program offers various business-related workshops in communities throughout the country.

GETTING ORGANIZED

If you scored a "2" or "1" on questions 1, 2, and 3, you need to *get motivated*. Businesses thrive when their owners are enthusiastic about what they're doing. But, all too often, an entrepreneur starts out with a terrific idea, only to lose momentum somewhere down the line. Staying motivated depends, in part, on being organized and scheduling your time wisely. Let's say you make and sell wooden toys, and you enthusiastically take orders for 15 items customers plan to give their kids for Christmas. You have four weeks to complete those orders, but all sorts of things come up: Your friend Sandy is giving a party Saturday night and instead of spending Saturday afternoon in your "toy shop," as you'd planned, you help Sandy buy party supplies, decorate, and cook. Then there's that U.S. Government paper due the week before Christmas. And your little brother just brought home a puppy that you'll have to housebreak (because your brother "just can't do it"). And you haven't started your holiday shopping yet . . . Slowly but surely, you give in to the "I'll make the toys tomorrow" excuse, and come December 24, you've got only five orders completed.

Numerous teen-run businesses go under because their owners don't know how to schedule their time. Try to set aside regular "work hours"—and consider them *sacred*. Figure out exactly how much time you'll need to spend on your business each day (or week), then chart it out on a master calendar. Pencil in study time, fun time, sports or other activities *around* your work schedule. Keep a list of tasks that need to be completed each week, and as you finish one, cross it off. Each time you complete a major job (or series of smaller tasks), reward yourself: go to a movie you've wanted to see, give yourself a new CD or a bottle of that new bubble bath your friends are raving about. By treating yourself well, by presenting yourself with little rewards, you'll motivate yourself and keep the momentum going.

Make sure your workspace and equipment are organized—you'll cut down on wasted steps. You need a place you can call your own, even if it's just a desk or work area in the corner of your basement. If you take lots of phone orders, or set up "service appointments" by phone, you'll need easy access to a telephone, and may want to invest in a hookup with your own personal line. Think about buying an inexpensive answering machine as well; it's likely your family won't appreciate taking a dozen or so customer calls a day. Also, an answering machine will keep you connected with your clients when you aren't at home, and you'll avoid losing business because someone got tired of trying to reach you.

Keep ledgers, notebooks, file folders, file cabinets and office necessities such as paper clips, rubber bands, pencils, and a typewriter or computer in your work area. You'll save time if you don't have to search the house for a paper clip, or run up two flights of stairs to use the computer.

LOOKING GOOD

Maintain a "professional appearance" when you're on the job. Customers tend to judge a business by the people who run it, and if you're appropriately dressed and groomed, you'll attract and impress potential customers. Even if yours is a "hands-on" business, such as a lawn-care company or a house-painting service, wear clean, pressed jeans and a clean, unripped tee, or reasonably clean coveralls to your appointments.

HIRING HOW-TOS

If your business grows to the point where you can't handle all the responsibilities yourself, consider delegating part of the work to family or friends (or even people you don't know). *Some* teens, like David Eilers (see his story, page 114), do such a booming business they have to hire part- or full-time employees. But taking on actual *employees* is a complicated business, according to John Bebris, National Program Manager of the Small Business Institute. "Laws regarding employees are very complex," says Bebris. "As an employer, you'll be responsible for all kinds of things like payroll accounting, disability insurance, social security withholding, etc. Once you get to the point where you need actual employees, you'll also need to consult a good accountant or an employee relations attorney who can keep you up-to-date on the very fast-moving changes in employee benefits laws."

Bebris advises teens to "sub-contract" work, that is, to pay someone to do work on a project-by-project basis. For example, if Terry of Terry's Terrific Tees decides to produce 50 percent more shirts during July and August, but can't handle the whole workload herself, she *could* "hire" her friend Chris to design some of the tees, and pay her $10 for each shirt she produces. Terry may ask Chris to do more work for her another time during the year, but that doesn't make Chris an "employee" of Terry's Terrific Tees—she's simply a "sub-contractor" or freelance worker. Terry's responsibility to Chris ends once she pays Chris for the work they agreed on; Terry needn't worry about payroll, social security or federal and state withholding tax, worker's compensation, or employee benefits. All she has to do is report, on IRS Form 1099, how much money she paid Chris from January 1 through December 31. Chris is then responsible for filing her own tax return and paying her self-employment tax.

Let's say you've decided to sub-contract a portion of your work, which will free you up to promote your business, make contacts, work on new marketing strategies. How do you find good workers?

Start by asking friends to join your venture. Advertise in your local newspaper. Put up notices on junior high, high school and college bulletin boards (some colleges have "placement centers"). Post signs at your church or temple and grocery store (get permission first).

When you interview, be specific about the job: what you want the person to do, what the hours are, the exact pay. You *may* want to put together an "application form," asking for previous job experience and references, etc.

Though hiring friends may seem ideal, remember that *some* friends don't work well together. It's difficult to tell a good friend what to do (tensions and hurt feelings may surface). You might find it's easier to give directions to casual acquaintances or people you have *no* personal relationship with. The same goes for hiring siblings: Your brother may turn out to be the most enthusiastic worker you'll find—or he may quit after a couple of days on the job because he resents taking orders from his sister!

LETTING GO

No employer likes having to let someone go—and it's doubly hard to "fire" a person if he or she is a friend. If one of your workers consistently turns in a poorly produced product or regularly fails to complete assigned tasks or show up for work, you owe it to yourself, your business, and even to your employee to take action. In this type of situation, try to avoid becoming emotional (though you will probably feel angry and frustrated). Calmly tell the employee that you've received numerous complaints from customers about his work, and that you can't efficiently run your business unless he does his fair share. Then give him a "grace period," two or three weeks to improve his work. Be specific, tell him exactly how he needs to improve his performance. Then suggest that you and he sit down on a specified date to evaluate his work again. At this point, your employee *may* decide to quit, or, he might get motivated and surprise you by doing a great job. If his performance doesn't improve, however, calmly explain that the situation isn't working out for either of you and your only choice is to look for someone else to handle his responsibilities.

Be sure to motivate your workers with *positive reinforcement.* If a worker spends hours delivering fliers to every home within a three-mile radius, compliment him on a job well done. Successful bosses know that praise prompts employees to do even better work. On the other hand, if one of your people isn't performing well, if he shows up late (or not at all), or produces a product that isn't up to your standards, you have to let him know you aren't satisfied with his work. But, whenever possible, lead off this conversation with a positive statement. For example, let's say you run a lawn service and your customers frequently complain that Johnny leaves patches of their lawn unmowed. Approach Johnny with, "I really like the way you trimmed Mrs. James' hedges last week. You're great at trimming but you need to pay more attention to your mowing." When you buffer criticism with a compliment, your worker will feel more inclined to follow your suggestions—and he won't feel as defensive as he might had you started out with your complaint.

RAKING IN THE PROFITS
When David Eilers was 10, he started mowing his neighbors' lawns. "I just wanted to earn a little money," says David, now 15. So many people started calling the Marietta, Georgia, boy that he had to "take the phone off the hook." And within a short time, David's Mowing Service—his motto is "We Can Cut It"— was born.

David's father bought him a $2,500 riding mower (he's since paid his dad back), and today the teen owns two pickup trucks and trailers, assorted power tools and several mowers, all purchased with profits from the business. In 1990, David's Mowing brought in $50,000 in revenue (up 39 percent from the previous year). By the end of 1992, he hopes to rake in approximately $100,000. He's also moved his business from his home to a portable building on land he leases. "My neighborhood isn't zoned for a business the size of mine," he explains. The building houses his mowing and office equipment.

When David first started out, he hired one of his dad's friends to help him on weekends. The next year, he says, "I had so much work, I had to hire two college students to work with me during the summer, eight hours a day, four or five days a week." During the past few years, David's employees have ranged from teenagers (his 17-year-old brother works for him) to men in their 20s and 30s. Today, he has three full-time employees, including a general manager who also handles customer service and sales ("He goes out and bids on jobs," explains David). David's mom oversees the day-to-day operations while he's in school: "She books appointments, answers the phone, does the paperwork, and makes sure all the jobs get done."

Hiring employees does pose problems, according to David. "We have to withhold their social security tax, provide workmen's compensation (in case an employee is injured on the job), and pay for special vehicle insurance since various people drive the trucks. My dad helped me figure out what I needed to know about workmen's comp and social security. He was part-owner of an advertising agency, so he knows about these things. He's my 'business expert.' "

David adds, "It's hard having employees who are twice as big as you—and two or three times your age." Hiring, and giving directions to people has gotten easier for David over time. He has learned more about running a business, and as a result, feels more confident about being a boss. "I asked my dad for advice about how to deal with employees—also, the more you do it, the better you become," says David, who has put together an application for prospective employees, asking for previous work experience and references. "Instead of just asking someone a few [verbal] questions, it helps to have a completed job application in front of you," he says.

David pays employees between $7 and $8 an hour (and he pays himself $7). He puts most of his revenue back into the company so it will continue to grow. "Right now, I'm working on expanding my client base," he says. "I want my business to be one of the five top landscaping companies in the Southeast by the time I'm 20."

15

Marketing Your Product, Promoting Your Business

Smart marketing and promotion strategies are the *keys* to growing a successful business. When you "market" a product or service, your first step is to determine "market share" and "market potential." You can do this by writing up a *customer profile—who* are you targeting your product or service to—and determining the size of the market—*how many* potential customers are there in your area? You should also know the number and strength of any competitors and estimate the *share* of business you'll take from them.

To define your market, ask yourself pertinent questions, such as the ones Terry, our tee-shirt vendor, asked herself before going into business:

1. Why is my tee-shirt (insert *your* product or service here) better than the ones already sold in my area?

- very good quality
- unique design
- competitive prices
- custom orders taken
- I'll "redo" work if a customer isn't satisfied

2. Who are my customers?

- grade school kids, teens and adults (but mostly teens and adults)
- people who attend craft fairs and art festivals
- people who buy from ABC Tee, but like the fact that I create custom designs (ABC doesn't)
- people who've bought my tees at the Bon Ton shop
- neighbors
- classmates

3. Where is my target market located?

- primarily at craft fairs (especially County Craft Fair, which draws twice as many people as other fairs)
- at the Bon Ton shop
- in my neighborhood
- at school

4. When are customers most likely to purchase my tees?

- during the summer (especially in July and August)
- just before Christmas (in November and early December)

5. Who are my competitors?

- other tee-shirt designers who sell at craft fairs
- ABC Tee

DO SOME MARKET RESEARCH

To make certain your product (or service) is in demand, ask people in your area whether a product like yours would appeal to them. Then ask 10 or 12 people to test your product: If you bake and sell cookies, give them samples to taste; if you design kids' toys, have parents try them out on their children. Be open to their suggestions—you may need to make a few variations on your original recipe, formulation or design before you come up with a crowd-pleaser.

Ask potential customers to compare your product (or service) to ones your competitors offer. What do they like about *your* product? What do they like about your competitors'? Which do they prefer and why?

LOCATION COUNTS

If you owned a restaurant, you'd want it to be smack in the heart of "downtown wherever," on a super-busy street where dozens of people walked by every hour. Likewise, as someone who's

starting a small business, you'll want to determine the ideal location for your operation. Obviously, if you work out of your home and take your product or service to your clients, you'll need to determine where your best *customer areas* are. Oren Jenkins found his "target market" in his own neighborhood—among the many elderly people who needed a reasonably priced lawn service. But what if Oren had lived in an area populated by young couples who were struggling to pay for child care and home mortgages—and couldn't afford to spend much money on lawn care? He would have had to analyze five or six other neighborhoods to determine which ones could provide the "upscale" clients he needed.

Similarly, Terry makes a good profit selling her tees at various craft fairs. *But,* some fairs draw heavier crowds than others, and Terry is wise to forgo a smaller fair, where she may sell only three or four tees in an afternoon, for a major one, where she can sell 10 tees in just a few hours.

PRICING

The price of a service or item is based on three basic product costs: direct materials, labor, and overhead (rent, cost of equipment). After you've determined what these costs total, you can then set a price that's both profitable and competitive. Pricing can be complicated, and you might want to consult an expert (a local businessperson or one of the volunteers at SCORE).

PROMOTING YOUR PRODUCT— AND YOUR BUSINESS

Once you've scoped out your target market, determined your market share, figured out where the majority of your customers are located, and set a price on your product or service, your next task is promoting—or advertising—your business.

Start by giving your company *an unusual or catchy name and slogan*—ones that will grab people's attention and stick in their minds. Terry's Terrific Tees is memorable because of the use of alliteration (words that all begin with the same letter or sound). David Eiler's mowing service got people to take notice with the clever slogan "We Can Cut It."

Next, decide how you're going to let people know that you exist, that your company has been born, and that you offer an exceptionally outstanding product or service. There are several methods for promoting your product and business:

Advertising. Use your local radio stations and newspapers. While the cost of TV ads is prohibitive for most small businesses, radio spots are often affordable. Call your local station and ask the cost of a 30-second or 60-second commercial (if your target market consists of teens, run your ad on a "rock" station; if you're aiming your product at adults, opt for an "easy-listening," or classical, or country western station).

Small-town newspapers also charge affordable rates for classified ads (you usually pay by the word or line), but metropolitan papers charge big bucks! If you do run an ad in the classifieds, be aware that it can get lost in the multitudes of other ads a paper typically crams on the page. You may want to save your money so you can afford a "display" ad, one that's boxed so it stands out. (You can usually choose a unique typeface or have your ad set in bold for more prominence.)

Business Cards. Zakia Andrews had business cards with the name of her lingerie-sales company, Simple Pleasures, a picture of a rose, and a phone number printed up to hand out to friends and other potential customers. Likewise, Morris Beyda invested in business cards when his company, Computers Simplified, started to take off. A good advertising tool, business cards lend a touch of professionalism to any venture, and you can post them in places such as restaurants, grocery stores, your school, church or temple. You can also tuck your card into bags along with a customer's purchase and receipt. That way, he'll know how to find you if he wants to order more of your product. Your local print shop can make up 50 to 100 cards, often for as little as $20 or $25.

Posters and Signs. Linda Menzies used her computer graphics skills to create posters advertising her Avon sales business (she posted them at strategic points around her college campus). If you're a computer graphics whiz, you too can design and run off posters on your computer. Or, you can design them freehand, using paint or felt-tip pens.

Here are some tips for creating appealing signs:

- Keep the signs simple. Include your company name and slogan, the product or service you're offering, and any special sales messages, such as "2 for the price of 1 Tee-Shirt Sale." If your prices are "the lowest in town," be sure to include that as well. And don't forget to include your phone number, so customers can place orders.
- Make sure your sign is readable: Use large "thick" letters; opt for color combinations that are both eye-catching and easy-to-read, such as black lettering on a hot pink or white background; and use only one or two colors—too many colors can create a confusing, chaotic look.

Include "phone tabs" for potential customers on your poster. Cut 10 to 12 short slits, or tabs, along a sheet of paper. Write your phone number and the name of your business on each tab. Using glue or tape, attach the top portion of the tab sheet to the bottom of your poster. Potential customers can easily tear off a tab—and won't have to go to the trouble of writing the info down.

Place your posters in your target market area, at community centers, groceries, churches and temples, schools, on telephone poles and tree trunks. Be sure to get permission from various organizations before placing signs on their premises; also, check with your county clerk to see whether your town or city has regulations regarding the size and placement of posters in public areas. Try to concentrate most of your posters in areas frequented by potential customers. For example, if you make and sell kids' clothes, place posters at church nursery schools, children's shoe stores, and at fast-food restaurants that cater to the toddler and pre-school crowd.

Fliers. These are similar to signs and posters because they include essentially the same info, but are printed on 8½″ × 11″ paper. Run multiple copies off on a copy machine, or on a word processor, or computer, then take your fliers door-to-door; slip them under doormats or cut out a "handle hole" so you can hang them on doorknobs. You can also hand out fliers at malls, your school, on the street (choose a busy one), at your grocery store, in parking lots, or at community events, such as fairs, concerts, basketball games. Be sure to check with town officials and organizations to make certain you can "advertise" on city or private premises. You *can* tuck fliers under car windshield wipers, but some people are annoyed by this (from a distance, a flier *could* be mistaken for a parking ticket!). Also, *do not* put fliers in mailboxes—it's illegal; only stamped mail delivered by the U.S. Postal Service can be placed in mailboxes.

Direct Mail. Send fliers or letters advertising your business by mail to people who are *most likely* to buy your product or service. Direct mail advertising can be costly—you pay not only for the fliers and envelopes (unless you fold the flier into thirds, staple or tape it shut, and write the customer's name and address on the back), but postage as well.

You may want to use direct mail advertising once your business gets off the ground and you know who your best customers are.

For example, if you sell items at a craft fair, keep a book handy and ask customers to pen in their names and addresses. Then you can send them fliers at a later date to let them know when you're having a sale or plan to be at a fair in their area.

Media Exposure. If a newspaper, radio or TV station, or regional or national magazine finds out about you and the terrific business you've started, they may want to *interview* you—and that can mean media exposure and increased sales.

When David Eilers won a "young entrepreneur's contest," his local paper ran a story about him. The story was picked up by other press organizations, and David was written up in *USA Today,* and appeared on CNN, NBC's *Today Show,* Channel One, and the teen TV show *Scratch.* "I've been successful partly because of all the publicity I've received," says David.

If you win an award for your achievement in business, be sure to alert your metropolitan and local newspapers. Chances are, they'll want to interview you, or run a blurb about your award. You can also send out *press releases* promoting your business. If there's something unusual or outstanding about your company (for example, you're the youngest house-painter in the county and you do an amazingly booming business, or you've invented a new product, or you regularly give a substantial part of your income to charity), you may want to send a press release to the media: local and metropolitan papers, radio and TV stations, and national teen magazines. A press release should be neatly typed and include your name and phone number, plus the name of your company and its address. The message should be simple but attention-getting, such as this:

Seattle, Washington: Sixteen-year-old Lynn Hollings operates one of the most successful cookie-baking operations in the county, selling her "Super Choco-Chip Cookies" to bakeries, restaurants and gourmet food shops. Last year, the teen brought in $25,000 in revenue.

But Lynn wanted to give *something back to her community, so this week she announced plans to donate 15 percent of her pre-tax profits to the Eastside Homeless Soup Kitchen, and provide 3 dozen cookies each week to the homeless families who eat at the shelter.*

"I feel so fortunate," says Lynn. "I have a great business, a wonderful family and friends—and I just wanted to give something to people who aren't as lucky as I am."

16

Savvy Sales Strategies

As a business owner, your primary job is to sell your product (or service)—and yourself.

As we've said before, customers often judge a business by the person who runs it, so it's essential that you project "professionalism" whenever you're on the job, on the phone, or dealing with customers in *any* way.

Start by dressing the part. If you're selling door-to-door, wear clean, neat clothes (a jacket will give you a businesslike appearance). You may want to invest in a blazer or tee with your company name embroidered on the pocket (people may feel more comfortable opening their doors to you if you have some sort of *visible identification*). If you're making a sales presentation to a local business to sell your wares or services, opt for "corporate dress": a jacket, slacks, conservative shirt and tie for guys; a jacket and dress, or jacket and skirt for girls.

Project a friendly, helpful attitude. You want people to *like* you—they'll be more inclined to buy your product or service. Oren Jenkins made a point of greeting his lawn care customers with a cheerful "good morning" or "good afternoon," and a smile—no matter what kind of mood he was in. As a result, his clients viewed him as "friendly and polite."

Practice listening, instead of talking. Top salespeople realize they'll alienate customers by trying to talk them into buying something they really don't need or want. Instead of pushing your product, *let the customer tell you* what he's looking for (A gift for his daughter? Something for himself?). If he isn't sure what he wants, or can't make up his mind, you can offer helpful suggestions.

Avoid hanging over your customers—they'll feel as though you're rushing them, or pressuring them into buying something. You'll sell more products if the customer feels relaxed, if he can take his time to look around and make an unhurried decision.

"The relaxed, casual nature of my Simple Pleasures parties helped me sell my products," says Zakia Andrews of her lingerie business. "Most of my customers knew each other, so the parties were a good opportunity for them to socialize. The fact that I served food and played music created an even more relaxing atmosphere." Zakia adds that her customers appreciated being able to buy lingerie without "feeling pressured," either by time constraints or by pushy salespeople. "The weren't rushing through a crowded store, weighed down by heavy bags and a coat, or waiting in long lines to pay," says Zakia. "At my parties, they could take their time to really examine the merchandise and make a decision. Almost everyone bought at least one piece of lingerie."

Follow the old adage, "The customer is always right"—even if he isn't! If a client isn't satisfied with your product or work, try to make him happy—within reason. Oren Jenkins had a policy of "redoing work if a client was unhappy with the way I'd trimmed his hedges, for example. My willingness to do something until I got it just right impressed my customers, and not only did they call me to do *more* work, they recommended me to their friends."

When you make a sale or finish a service job, take time to thank your customers for their business. If you work at your clients' homes while they're away (as a pet-sitter, housekeeper, lawn-care person) and you aren't able to thank them in person, call the following day to ask if they were pleased with your work, or send a thank-you note by mail.

MORE SMART SELLING TIPS

- Do you plan to sell your product (or service) door-to-door? You'll catch the majority of people at home in the early evening and right after dinner. Avoid knocking on doors during the dinner hour (5:30 P.M. to 7 P.M.); families are too busy at that time to be receptive to your sales pitch. Likewise, don't canvass a neighborhood after 8 P.M.; people simply won't want to be disturbed.
- No one at home? Leave your business card or a flier under the doormat or hang a flier on the doorknob.

    If someone *does* answer your knock, keep your sales pitch short (and be sure to smile). Tell the person who you are, what you do ("I'm washing windows in your neighborhood this week") and give a rough estimate of your prices. If the person says he isn't interested in your services, ask if you can leave a flier or card—just in case he needs something later on.
- If you sell a service or products to *other* businesses (for example, you peddle your handmade jewelry to small boutiques and trendier department stores), practice your "sales presentation" before meeting with the store owner or buyer. Be sure to bring samples, or at the very least, photos of your work. Leave a sample (or photo) with the store rep—that way she'll remember you and your work (clip a business card with your name, address and phone number onto samples, or pen info onto the backs of photos).

    Before calling on businesses, determine the price you'll need to charge in order to make a profit. For example, if a store offers to pay $8 for each tee shirt you've designed, and you've paid between $2 and $4 for the plain shirts, then put two hours into designing them, you'll make little—if any—profit. You'd be better off selling your tees for $20 or more at craft fairs.

If, on the other hand, the store pays you $15 for each tee (they'll sell them for $25 or $30), you can expect to make a profit of $8 to $10, which may be acceptable during the winter when craft fairs are few and far between.

TRICKS OF THE TRADE

You can attract new customers and boost sales with these popular "sales promotion" techniques:

Offer a "gift." Give buyers a freebie with any $25 purchase. If you sell baked goods, and a customer buys a $25 gift basket, present him with a bag of eight cookies. Post a sign advertising "free gift with purchase" on your booth or business premises.

Give first-time customers a price break. If you usually charge $30 to cut clients' lawns and trim their hedges, distribute fliers to potential customers announcing an *introductory price* of $20.

Give away free samples. Do you run a candy company? Arrange samples on a tray for browsers to taste. If you bake and sell cookies, cakes or muffins, cut your goods into half-inch pieces and arrange on a sample tray.

Present coupons. Staple them to posters or write them on fliers, offering a 10 percent to 20 percent discount on your product or service.

Offer prizes. If you sell your wares at "parties," such as the ones Zakia Andrews held for her Simple Pleasures business, buy two or three inexpensive gifts to give to people who win party games or make the most purchases. Zakia noted on her posters and in fliers that "door prizes will be given."

FOR THESE SISTERS, SELLING IS A FAMILY AFFAIR

Selling is second nature for the Keppler sisters of Sheboygan, Wisconsin. Now in their 20s, Abby, Sarah, and Becky Keppler sold Avon products during high school and used the profits to pay for most of their college expenses.

Abby got into the business first. "I was looking for a part-time job that would allow me to have time for extracurricular activities and go on family vacations during the summer," she says. "I didn't want a fixed schedule. I talked to my mom, who's an Avon Representative, and she got me started." (Technically, Becky helped her mother, Maxine, sell the products.)

Abby, then 16, sold the products at school and also covered a "territory"—an area of homes in an adjacent neighborhood. Business was brisk, and she eventually had difficulty managing everything in her hectic schedule when she started getting ready for college. That's when Sarah got involved, helping Abby deliver catalogs and orders to customers, and taking phone calls when Abby wasn't at home (Abby paid Sarah for her work). By the time Abby left for college, 15-year-old Sarah was ready to take over the business. And when Sarah moved to Milwaukee two years later to attend the University of Wisconsin, Becky, 15, became chief salesperson.

"We usually weren't all selling at once," explains Becky, "but at one time we did cover three territories, each with 100 people in it." The sisters pooled their profits into one general account, under their mom's name, which simplified bookkeeping procedures.

The Keppler sisters all agree that selling Avon taught them a great deal about responsibility, money management, and dealing with people. And one, Abby, has used the experience to get on the fast track in a sales career. "Because of my Avon experience, I was hired right out of college to be sales manager of a large subscription television firm in Chicago," she says. "The Avon experience was a big plus on my résumé."

What sales strategies do the Kepplers offer to young entrepreneurs?

"*Listen to your customer,*" *advises Sarah.* "*Let her talk, and you'll learn what she wants and needs. Don't try to persuade her to buy something just because it's new or because you like it.*"

The sisters also emphasize that if you're selling door-to-door, it's important to leave something tangible at each home—a business card, a flier, or a brochure. "*We always left a catalog,*" says Sarah, "*even if the person said she wasn't interested in buying anything. Eventually, she'd flip through the catalog and find something she did want to buy. When you leave a customer alone with a catalog, they're free to make a decision without feeling pressured.*"

"*Be sure to 'follow up' on every call,*" advise the sisters. "*We tried to get each person's name and phone number, then we'd call (or stop by) at a later date to see if they needed something. In door-to-door sales, 'follow up' is one of the biggest keys to being successful.*"

17

Easy Accounting How-Tos

Every business owner needs to know what his "cash flow" is—
how much money *comes in* and *goes out* of his business every day.

By keeping accurate records, you'll know exactly how your
business is doing: Are you making a profit? Taking a loss? You also
need to keep track of income (the money you make) and expenses (the money you spend on business-related items and
services) for income tax purposes.

Start by investing in a simple bookkeeping ledger, or just dupli-
cate the "cash flow record" below. On each business day, record
the *date*, a description of *why* you received or spent money, the
amount of money received or spent, and the *cash you have on
hand* after you subtract your expenses from your income. Here's
a one-week cash flow record we charted for Terry's Terrific Tees:

WEEKLY CASH FLOW

DATE	EXPLANATION	INCOME	EXPENSES	CASH ON HAND
6/2				$100
6/5	Sold 4 tees	$80		$180
6/6	Bought paints		$10	$170
6/7	Sold 5 tees	$100		$270
6/8	Bought 20 plain tees		$40	$230
6/10	Sold 3 tees	$60		$260

(Terry started with $100 profits from the preceding week)

Open a checking account at your local bank and pay for all expenses by check; that way, you'll have proof you've paid for something. Also, ask for a receipt from wholesalers or other vendors. Keep cancelled checks and receipts in a folder labelled "expenses" (a folder for each month in a calendar year is a good idea).

When you *sell* a product or service, give the customer a receipt (keep a copy for yourself). Office supply stores carry "receipt pads" that make instant duplicates (some even work *without* messy carbons). Keep all your sales receipt duplicates in a folder.

Whenever possible, ask customers to pay with cash or by check at the time they buy your product or service. If you allow customers to pay later or "on time" (stretching payments over a few weeks or a month), you must include an "accounts receivable" column in your cash flow record. Write down the amount the person owes you under "accounts receivable." When he pays his bill, cross off the amount and record it under the "income" heading.

If *you* arrange to pay a wholesaler or vendor at a later date, record the amount under a column entitled "accounts payable." When you pay your bill, cross out the amount and record it under the "expenses" heading.

Items you should list in the "expenses" column include office supplies, phone bills, materials, merchandise, advertising and promotion costs, postage and car expenses. Keep receipts for *all* these expenditures; depending on the amount of your income and how much money you dole out on business-related expenses, you *may* be able to declare some as deductions on your tax form. For more info, call the IRS (also, check out IRS Publications No. 535, *Business Expenses* and No. 917, *Business Use of a Car.*

If you sub-contract work on a project-by-project basis (paying your little brother or a friend to deliver fliers, for example), simply record the amount in the "expenses" column on your cash flow record.

If you hire *employees,* you'll have to keep detailed payroll records, charting salaries and withholding tax (let a qualified accountant advise you on payroll records).

To avoid having to search through piles of paper on your desk, keep all records organized by month and year in one file cabinet so you have easy access to them (especially important come tax time!).

18

Business Problems? Here's Help!

Ideally, your business will thrive, you'll attract customers by the dozens (or hundreds!), and you'll turn a handsome profit. But what if your business grows slowly? Or, after a great start (or even a spectacular first year) you begin to lose customers or your profits dwindle?

Even the most successful business owners face *some* problems now and then. The key to overcoming those difficulties is to understand *why* they're occurring, then figure out the best ways to "cure" the problems.

Here's a sample of the business woes you may face and how to deal with them:

Problem: Your profits are minimal.

Solution: Determine whether the price you've set for your product or service is too low. For example, if you charge a flat fee of $30 to wash windows, you may do very well tending to houses that have a minimum number of windows. But houses with large, numerous or hard-to-reach windows will cost you time—and money. In this type of situation, tailor your fee to fit the project. For a house with many windows, double your rate (commercial window washers charge between $100 and $150 to clean windows inside and out on a medium-sized house!).

If you make and sell a product, add up the cost of your materials and the amount of time you spend making an item; your profit should exceed the cost by 40 to 50 percent. If it doesn't, either make your product for *less,* or sell it for *more* to increase your income.

Problem: You don't have enough customers.

Solution: Reevaluate your location. If you sell your product at craft fairs, are you hitting the biggest ones—the fairs that attract "upscale" clients who are likely to spend more freely on gift items? Do you own a lawncare service (or housepainting or bicycle repair company)? Your own neighborhood may not be a good source of clients. Scout out other, more affluent neighborhoods or expand your business into surrounding communities.

Reanalyze your "target market" in relation to your product or service. Your adorable tees *may* hold greater appeal for little kids than for the teens you're marketing to. Try selling to parents and grandparents of preschoolers and grade-school kids.

Increase your customer base by stepping up your advertising and promotion campaigns. When business is slow, deliver more fliers to target market homes; post signs in places where your *ideal* customer will see them.

Offer "incentives," such as the ones we mentioned in Chapter 16: a free gift with purchase; a low introductory price; a free sample.

Problem: Your regular customers aren't calling you or buying your product anymore.

Solution: Do some market "re-research." Call 10 or 12 of these people or send them a questionnaire (include a stamped, self-addressed envelope) and ask for "suggestions" on how you can improve your product or service.

You're likely to get some good advice on how you can make your product better, or ways you can deliver higher quality service. You'll also discover *why* you're losing clients. For instance, maybe the slow economy has forced Mr. Jones to cut back on expenditures, including the $30 he pays you to tend his lawn. In that case, you might offer to give him a "discount" for a few months; or suggest that you care for his lawn once or twice a month, instead of once a week.

Or let's say several of your customers tell you they're "watching their weight"—so they're not buying your double-fudge chocolate chip cookies. Consider developing a reduced-calorie, reduced-fat cookie for dieters.

Problem: You've got tons of orders for your handmade jewelry, but not enough time to make all the items.

Solution: Create jewelry designs that require less work time, or hire a talented friend to help you make your bracelets, necklaces and earrings (she can copy your originals, or create her own designs). Likewise, when your lawncare jobs drastically cut into study, family (and sleep!) time, sub-contract some of your work to a reliable friend or acquaintance.

Have a business problem you can't solve? Contact the experts at SCORE (the Service Corps of Retired Executives) for free advice. To connect with a SCORE volunteer in your area, call 1-800-U-ASK-SBA.

19

Establishing Credit

Now that you're earning money—whether you're a small business owner, or you work for somebody else—it's a good idea to think about establishing a "credit rating."

By becoming a "good credit risk" as a teen, you'll be on your way to being viewed as a good credit risk as an adult, and you'll be more likely to get financing for a first home, a car loan, or money to start (or expand) your business.

You can establish credit by opening a charge account at a major department store. Most stores issue cards to people 18 or older; if you're under 18, one of your parents may apply for the card and allow you to co-sign the account. When you fill out the credit card application, list your income (from your part-time job or your business), as well as your "assets," the money you have in your savings and checking accounts, CDs, stocks, bonds, or trust funds. You may also want to list any business-related items of value that you possess—a computer, word processor, power mower, expensive camera equipment, power tools.

Once you receive your charge card, begin by charging one or two small items each month. Buy things you actually need—underwear, socks, sweaters—and pay your bill as soon as you receive it. If you don't pay your bill promptly (most stores give you a certain number of days to pay), you'll be charged interest—usually 18 percent to 19 percent annually on the unpaid amount (some states require lower interest charges, others higher).

After six months of charging items on your store account, apply for another department store charge card, and possibly a gasoline credit card. Once you've accumulated two or three cards—and have paid your bills promptly each month—you may want to apply for a "bank card." Numerous banks issue cards under the trade names VISA and MasterCard. You can use these cards at many stores and other businesses, hotels, and restaurants. When you apply for a bank card, be sure to list your employment history, income and assets, *plus* the store and gasoline credit cards you already hold because most banks prefer to issue cards to people with established credit.

Some banks charge an annual membership fee (ranging from $20 to $75). Others waive the fee for the first year in order to attract applicants. If you pay your bill on time each month (you usually have 25 days), you won't be charged a finance fee. If you pay only part of your bill each month, you'll be charged interest (19-plus percent annually) on the unpaid amount.

Before applying for a bank card, check out four or five banks in your area; ask about the annual interest rates and membership fees. Some banks offer better deals than others—lower interest rates, minimal membership fees. Make sure the bank allows you at least 25 days to pay your bill in full before charging interest— a few banks start charging interest the moment you make a purchase!

CHARGING SMARTS

"Paying with plastic," rather than writing a check or handing over cash, is so easy people often get into serious debt before they realize it. Here are some tips for smart charging:

- Whenever you use your charge card, be it a store, gas or bank card, write down the amount you're charging. Keep a little notepad in your purse or pocket, and at the end of the day (or week), you'll have a running tab of charges that you can reconcile with the amount of money you have in the bank.

- Use your cards only for necessities, or in a pinch. For example, say your car needs two new tires, and you don't have the cash. You rely on your car for your business or to get to your job, so new tires are an absolute necessity. You can charge your tires and pay off the amount over time.

- Pay your bills immediately. If you purchase a "sale" item, thinking you're getting a great deal, but then take six months to pay the full amount, your finance charge may end up exceeding the cost of the item *before* it went on sale! Also, if you pay only the minimum amount due on your charge account each month, and keep making *new* charges, you'll soon be in over your head.

- If you aren't able to make the minimum payment—or your full payment will be late—call the customer service department (the number is listed on your monthly statements). Explain that you're temporarily strapped for cash and ask if you can work out a payment plan. This way, you may avoid having your late payment—or non-payment— reported to a credit bureau (see "Your Credit Record," page 141).

- Keep your credit cards neatly organized in your wallet. Always make sure a sales clerk hands back your card with your receipt. Also, ask for the "carbons" from the receipt, and tear them up once you get home. If you discover you've *lost* a card (or it's been stolen), *immediately* notify the organization that issued the card (call the number listed on your monthly statement). If an unauthorized person makes purchases using your card, you are usually responsible for paying the first $50 charged.

YOUR CREDIT RECORD

Once you receive a credit card (or get a loan, for that matter), your credit is tracked by three major credit bureaus: TRW, Trans Union and Equifax, Inc. These agencies chart your credit carefully, recording everything from whether you pay your bills on time to any late or non-payments. If you pay your bills late or not at all, or your account has been turned over to a collection agency, you'll be regarded as a "bad credit risk," and will have trouble getting credit cards from other issuers or obtaining a loan. To get a copy of your credit rating or report (which is, by the way, available to just about everyone, from banks to credit card issuers to potential employers!), you'll need to write to the various credit bureaus. Most charge a $20 fee for a report; some provide them free.

EPILOGUE

Congratulations! If you've reached this page, chances are you've read through every chapter of this book, discovering the tried-and-true techniques for finding and succeeding at a summer or afterschool job, or, you've learned the ins and outs of starting your own business. Now, the rest is up to you. Put what you've learned into action: go to work—literally—and become one of America's Enterprising Teens. We wish you all the best!

Linda
Oren
Rickell

RESOURCES

Need more info on putting together a résumé or finding a job? Stop by your local library and ask the *reference librarian* to direct you toward books about jobs and career opportunities. Also check the bulletin boards at libraries—many post jobs in the community or county.

Interested in learning more about economics or business basics? Ask your school principal or business teacher if the school participates in the economic education programs developed by the Joint Council on Economic Education for Students, K-12. If it doesn't, suggest they contact the JCEE at 1-800-338-1192 to set up a program.

Want to participate in an intensive, in-depth seminar on entrepreneurship? Apply for Wharton's EntreCon High School Annual Conference on Entrepreneurship. For a fee schedule and more info about the four-day workshop, write to EntreCon 1992, Wharton Undergraduate Division, Suite 1100, Steinberg Hall-Dietrich Hall, Philadelphia, PA 19104-6357.

Interested in joining a young entrepreneur's club? Write to Busines$ Kids/America's Future, 301 Almeria Ave., Suite 330, Coral Gables, FL 33134. You can join Busines$ Kids for an annual membership fee of $9.95. As a member, you'll receive a newsletter, be eligible to attend various workshops, and have access to the club's toll-free hotline, which offers advice regarding business problems. In addition, the organization offers The Busines$ Kit, which consists of books and tapes detailing how to start and run a business, plus business cards, stationery and an appointment book. To order, send $49.95, plus $8.50 postage and handling (check or money order) to the above address; or call 1-800-852-4544.

Need help running or expanding your operation? Have questions or business-related problems you can't solve? Call SCORE, the Service Corps of Retired Executives, a volunteer branch of the U.S. Small Business Administration (SBA). SCORE will team you with an expert who can give *free* advice about almost every facet of starting and running a business. To locate your nearest SBA office (and a SCORE volunteer), call 1-800-U ASK SBA.

The SBA offers many helpful pamphlets, books and videocassettes on entrepreneurship. To order the ones listed below, write to SBA Publications, P.O. Box 30, Denver, CO 80201-0030. Make your check or money order payable in U.S. dollars to: U.S. Small Business Administration. For two or more items, add $1 for domestic shipping and handling. To cover extra handling costs for shipments outside of U.S., add 25 percent to your total order. Include your name, street address, city, state, and ZIP Code, plus your daytime phone number (with area code). Be sure to also include code numbers for each publication you order.

Videotapes
Marketing: Winning Customers with a Workable Plan provides a step-by-step approach on how to write the best possible marketing plan for your business plus best methods to determine customer needs—and more; $30 (VT1).

The Business Plan: Your Roadmap to Success provides the essentials of developing a business plan that will help lead you to capital, growth, and profitability; $30 (VT2).

Publications
Ideas Into Dollars identifies the main challenges in product development and provides a list of resources to help inventors and innovators take their ideas into the marketplace; $2 (PI1).

Avoiding Patent, Trademark and Copyright Problems shows how to avoid infringing on the rights of others and the importance of protecting your own rights; $1 (PI2).

Understanding Cash Flow explains how to plan for the movement of cash through your business and thus plan for future requirements; $1 (FM4).

Budgeting in a Small Service Firm demonstrates how to set up and keep sound financial records; 50 cents (FM8).

Record-Keeping in a Small Business provides basic advice on record-keeping; $1 (FM10).

Pricing Your Products and Services Profitably shows you how to price your products so you make money, plus offers advice on various pricing techniques and when to use them; $1 (FM13).

Planning and Goal Setting for Small Business demonstrates proven management techniques to help you plan for success; 50 cents (MP6).

Checklist for Going into Business is a must if you're thinking of starting a business—it highlights important factors you should know before you begin; $1 (MP12).

The Business Plan for Home-based Business; $1 (MP15).

Developing a Strategic Business Plan; $1 (MP21).

Techniques for Problem Solving demonstrates how to identify and solve business problems; $1 (MP23).

Marketing for Small Business: An Overview provides marketing concepts and an extensive bibliography of sources covering the subject of marketing; $1 (MT2).

Researching Your Market (inexpensive ways to gather facts about your customer base and how to expand it); $1 (MT8).

Advertising shows how you can effectively advertise your products and services; $1 (MT11).

Employees: How to Find and Pay Them; $1 (PM2).

The Internal Revenue Service offers all sorts of free pamphlets and publications related to tax topics. Stop by your local IRS office and check out the following:

No. 334, *Tax Guide for Small Business.*

No. 910, *Guide to Free Tax Services.*

No. 533, *Self-employment Tax.*

No. 535, *Business Expenses.*

No. 583, *Taxpayers Starting a Business.*

No. 911, *Tax Information for Direct Sellers.*

No. 917, *Business Use of a Car.*

No. 1, *Your Rights as a Taxpayer.*

No. 17, *Your Federal Income Tax* (for individuals).

*Interested in becoming an Avon sales Representative? You're eligible if you're 18 or older. Just write to: Avon Products, Inc., 1 (800) 858-8000 (Be sure to include your name, address and complete phone number.)

Good Reads

Check out these other helpful MasterMedia books for everything from advice on marketing your product to upping your self-esteem. Have your local bookseller order these smart reads, or call 1-800-334-8232 for ordering how-tos:

Positively Outrageous Service: New & Easy Ways to Win Customers for Life, by T. Scott Gross, $14.95 (paper).

The Confidence Factor: How Self-Esteem Can Change Your Life, by Judith Briles, $9.95 (paper).

Taking Control of Your Life: The Secrets of Successful, Enterprising Women, by Gail Blanke and Kathleen Walas, $17.95.

Criticism in Your Life: How to Give It—How to Take It—How to Make It Work for You, by Dr. Deborah Bright, $9.95 (paper).

Beyond Success: How Volunteer Service Can Help You Begin Making a Life Instead of Just a Living, by John F. Reynolds III, and Eleanor Reynolds, C.B.E., $9.95 (paper).

Real Beauty . . . Real Women, by Kathleen Walas, $19.50.

Balancing Acts! Juggling Love, Work, Family, and Recreation, by Susan S. Stautberg and Marcia Worthing, $12.95.

Real Life 101: The Graduate's Guide to Survival, by Susan Kleinman, $9.95.

Breathing Space: Living and Working at a Comfortable Pace in a Sped-up Society, by Jeff Davidson, $10.95.

ABOUT THE AUTHORS

LINDA MENZIES, 21, worked at a screen printing company and then started her own graphics design firm. She attends Pratt University and lives in Miami Beach, Florida.

OREN S. JENKINS, 19, ran his own lawn service operation and has worked at increasingly responsible jobs at Kings Amusement Park. He is a student at Ohio Wesleyan University and lives in Cincinnati, Ohio.

RICKELL RAE FISHER, 20, has worked on an assembly line, in a department store, and as an Avon College Representative. She attends Indiana University of Pennsylvania, which is in her home town.

Additional copies of *A Teen's Guide to Business: The Secrets to a Successful Enterprise* may be ordered by sending a check for $7.95 (please add the following for postage and handling: $2.00 for the first copy, $1.00 for each added copy) to:

MasterMedia Limited
19 East 89th Street
New York, NY 10128
(212) 260-5600
(800) 334-8232
(212) 348-2020 (fax)

OTHER MASTERMEDIA BOOKS

THE PREGNANCY AND MOTHERHOOD DIARY: Planning the First Year of Your Second Career, by Susan Schiffer Stautberg, is the first and only undated appointment diary that shows how to manage pregnancy and career. ($12.95 spiralbound)

CITIES OF OPPORTUNITY: Finding the Best Place to Work, Live and Prosper in the 1990's and Beyond, by Dr. John Tepper Marlin, explores the job and living options for the next decade and into the next century. This consumer guide and handbook, written by one of the world's experts on cities, selects and features forty-six American cities and metropolitan areas. ($13.95 paper, $24.95 cloth)

THE DOLLARS AND SENSE OF DIVORCE, The Financial Guide for Women, by Judith Briles, is the first book to combine practical tips on overcoming the legal hurdles with planning before, during and after divorce ($10.95 paper)

OUT THE ORGANIZATION: New Career Opportunities for the 1990's, by Madeleine and Robert Swain, is written for the millions of Americans whose jobs are no longer safe, whose companies are not loyal and who face futures of uncertainty. It gives advice on finding a new job or starting your own business. ($12.95 paper)

AGING PARENTS AND YOU: A Complete Handbook to Help You Help Your Elders Maintain a Healthy, Productive and Independent Life, by Eugenia Anderson-Ellis and Marsha Dryan, is a complete guide to providing care to aging relatives. It gives practical advice and resources to the adults who are helping their elders lead productive and independent lives. ($9.95 paper)

CRITICISM IN YOUR LIFE: How to Give It, How to Take It, How to Make It Work for You, by Dr. Deborah Bright, offers practical advice, in an upbeat, readable and realistic fashion, for turning criticism into control. Charts and diagrams guide the reader into managing criticism from bosses, spouses, children, friends, neighbors and in-laws. ($9.95 paper, $17.95 cloth)

BEYOND SUCCESS: How Volunteer Service Can Help You Begin Making a Life Instead of Just a Living, by John F. Raynolds III and Eleanor Raynolds, C.B.E., is a unique how-to book targeted to business and professional people considering volunteer work, senior citizens who wish to fill leisure time meaningfully and students trying out various career options. The book is filled with interviews with celebrities, CEOs and average citizens who talk about the benefits of service work. ($9.95 paper, $19.95 cloth)

MANAGING IT ALL: Time-Saving Ideas for Career, Family, Relationships and Self, by Beverly Benz Treuille and Susan Schiffer Stautberg, is written for women who are juggling careers and families. Over two hundred career women (ranging from a TV anchorwoman to an investment banker) were interviewed. The book contains many humorous anecdotes on saving time and improving the quality of life for self and family. ($9.95 paper)

REAL LIFE 101: The Graduate's Guide to Survival, by Susan Kleinman, supplies welcome advice to those facing "real life" for the first time, focusing on work, money, health and how to deal with freedom and responsibility. ($9.95 paper)

YOUR HEALTHY BODY, YOUR HEALTHY LIFE: How to Take Control of Your Medical Destiny, by Donald B. Louria, M.A., provides precise advice and strategies that will help you to live a long and healthy life. Learn also about nutrition, exercise, vitamins and medication, as well as how to control risk factors for major diseases. ($12.95 paper)

THE CONFIDENCE FACTOR: How Self-Esteem Can Change Your Life, by Judith Briles, is based on a nationwide survey of six thousand men and women. Briles explores why women so often feel a lack of self-confidence and have a poor opinion of themselves. She offers step-by-step advice on becoming the person you want to be. ($9.95 paper, $18.95 cloth)

THE SOLUTION TO POLLUTION: 101 Things You Can Do to Clean Up Your Environment, by Laurence Sombke, offers step-by-step techniques on how to conserve more energy, start a recycling center, choose biodegradable products and proceed with individual environmental cleanup projects. ($7.95 paper)

TAKING CONTROL OF YOUR LIFE: The Secrets of Successful Enterprising Women, by Gail Blanke and Kathleen Walas, is based on the authors' professional experience with Avon Products' Women of Enterprise Awards, given each year to outstanding women entrepreneurs. The authors offer a specific plan to help you gain control over your life and include business tips and quizzes as well as beauty and lifestyle information. ($17.95 cloth)

SIDE-BY-SIDE STRATEGIES: How Two-Career Couples Can Thrive in the Nineties, by Jane Hershey Cuozzo and S. Diane Graham, describes how two-career couples can learn the difference between competing with a spouse and becoming a supportive power partner. Published in hardcover as *Power Partners.* ($10.95 paper)

DARE TO CONFRONT! How to Intervene When Someone You Care About Has an Alcohol or Drug Problem, by Bob Wright and Deborah George Wright, shows the reader how to use the step-by-step methods of professional interventionists to motivate drug-dependent people to accept the help they need. ($17.95 cloth)

WORK WITH ME! How to Make the Most of Office Support Staff, by Betsy Lazary, shows how to find, train, and nurture the "perfect" assistant and how best to utilize your support staff professionals. ($9.95 paper)

MANN FOR ALL SEASONS: Wit and Wisdom from The Washington Post's *Judy Mann,* by Judy Mann, shows the columnist at her best as she writes about women, families and the politics of the women's revolution. ($9.95 paper, $19.95 cloth)

THE SOLUTION TO POLLUTION IN THE WORKPLACE, by Laurence Sombke, Terry M. Robertson and Elliot M. Kaplan, supplies employees with everything they need to know about cleaning up their workplace, including recycling, using energy efficiently, conserving water and buying recycled products and nontoxic supplies. ($9.95 paper)

THE ENVIRONMENTAL GARDENER: The Solution to Pollution for Lawns and Gardens, by Laurence Sombke, focuses on what each of us can do to protect our endangered plant life. A practical sourcebook and shopping guide. ($8.95 paper)

THE LOYALTY FACTOR: Building Trust in Today's Workplace, by Carol Kinsey Goman, Ph.D., offers techniques for restoring commitment and loyalty in the workplace. ($9.95 paper)

DARE TO CHANGE YOUR JOB—AND YOUR LIFE, by Carole Kanchier, Ph.D., provides a look at career growth and development throughout the life cycle. ($10.95 paper)

MISS AMERICA: In Pursuit of the Crown, by Ann-Marie Bivans, is an authorized guidebook to the Pageant, containing eyewitness accounts, complete historical data, and a realistic look at the trials and triumphs of potential Miss Americas. ($27.50 cloth)

POSITIVELY OUTRAGEOUS SERVICE: New and Easy Ways to Win Customers for Life, by T. Scott Gross, identifies what the consumers of the nineties really want and how businesses can develop effective marketing strategies to answer those needs. ($14.95 paper)

BREATHING SPACE: Living and Working at a Comfortable Pace in a Sped-Up Society, by Jeff Davidson, helps readers to handle information and activity overload and gain greater control over their lives. ($10.95 paper)

TWENTYSOMETHING: Managing and Motivating Today's New Work Force, by Lawrence J. Bradford, Ph.D., and Claire Raines, M.A., examines the work orientation of the younger generation, offering managers in businesses of all kinds a practical guide to better understanding and supervising their young employees. ($22.95 cloth)

BALANCING ACTS! Juggling Love, Work, Family and Recreation, by Susan Schiffer Stautberg and Marcia L. Worthing, provides strategies to achieve a balanced life by reordering priorities and setting realistic goals. ($12.95 paper)

STEP FORWARD: Sexual Harassment in the Workplace, by Susan L. Webb, teaches the reader all the basic facts about sexual harassment as well as furnishing procedures to help stop it. ($9.95 paper)

THE LIVING HEART BRAND NAME SHOPPER'S GUIDE, by Michael E. DeBakey, M.D., Antonio M. Gotto, Jr., M.D., D.Phil., Lynne W. Scott, M.A., R.D./L.D., and John P. Foreyt, Ph.D., lists brand name supermarket products that are low in fat, saturated fatty acids, and cholesterol. ($12.50 paper)

REAL BEAUTY . . . REAL WOMEN: A Workbook for Making the Best of Your Own Good Looks, by Kathleen Walas, National Beauty and Fashion Director of Avon Products, offers expert advice on beauty and fashion to women of all ages and ethnic backgrounds. ($19.50 cloth)

MANAGING YOUR CHILD'S DIABETES, by Robert Wood Johnson IV, Sale Johnson, Casey Johnson, and Susan Kleinman, brings help to families trying to understand diabetes and control its effects. ($10.95 paper, $18.95 cloth)